The Overcome Story

Child: **Who are we?**

Parent: We are the Overcome people, the people of the Overcome. Our people, black people of Africa, have been made to suffer much, and out of this suffering our new character has been forged. We are by nature, definition, and character the people who can and will Overcome every, any and all negatives, seen and unseen, placed in our way.

Child: **Where did we come from?**

Parent: We came from Africa where we had already developed great civilizations; gave the world its moral code, the Ten Commandments; its principles of mathematics, especially in geometry; its first formal philosophy. We came from the land of St. Augustine of Hippo, who developed the framework for all Christian theology; from the continent with the great universities of Timbuktu; the continent of the wonderful pyramids of Giza, of Shaka Zulu and other great kings with powerful kingdoms.

Child: **How did we get so low?**

Parent: In our greatness, we foolishly became complacent and stopped trying to develop further. We then went into a hiatus or sleep for several centuries while others came and took our concepts, our religions, our moral codes, our philosophies and techniques, expanding upon them, while forcing us to forget our past greatness. They then took our lands; later they would take us from the land as they developed the sinful black slave trade. They told deliberate lies about the origins of humanity and origins of civilizations, even though their own science now confirms that we are the parents of all living mankind because the genes [DNA] of an African mother are to be found in every man, woman and child on earth.

Child: **Why do we celebrate this season?**

Parent: For centuries we were oppressed and dehumanized as a people. We were described negatively and given demeaning names. But, when the time was right, the cosmic powers brought their forces to bear, and one of our own was sacrificed for us. His name was Martin. Then, he was lifted up. All he stood for, all he worked to accomplish, and all he died for, was vindicated and lifted up. So, we celebrate his day of sacrifice. We celebrate his death and how his consequent elevation validates our new status as overcomers. For not even death could stop him from being vindicated.

Child: **What does the Overcome demand of us?**

Parent: Overcome Day, April 4, reminds us that we are Overcomers by nature. It reminds us that though hurts and pains abide, it is now our nature to overcome them, and not be overcome by them. We know this because our foreparents overcame the Middle Passage. They overcame slavery, and all the hurts since slavery. And out of all this suffering came our new character description as Overcomers, who can, will and must overcome whatever barriers, whatever negatives, whatever obstacles are placed in our way. Martin Luther King's elevation, after death, confirms that even death cannot stop Overcomers. And that is the reason we celebrate, exult, and thank our foreparents for bequeathing us our new character as Overcomers.

Child: **Why do we eat grits with this nice dinner?**

Parent: While we were subdued, we built monuments, businesses and all kinds of institutions for others. The grits represent mortar, the mortar we use to build our own life-giving, life-supporting and life-sustaining institutions.

The Overcome:
A Black Passover

The Rev. Dr. Martin Luther King, Jr.

Drawing by Ronald Xavier Roberson
Copyright©C. H. Fairfax Company

The Overcome:
A Black Passover

by

Peter W. D. Bramble, Ph.D.

C. H. Fairfax Company Publishers

Columbia Ω Maryland Ω Baltimore

Copyright©1989 by Peter W. D. Bramble, Ph.D.

All rights reserved. No part of this book may be reproduced or transmitted in any form by any means, electronic or mechanical, including photocopying and recording, or by any information storage or retrieval system, without permission in writing from the publisher

Published by C. H. Fairfax Company, Inc.
Paul F. Evans, Publisher
P. O. Box 502
Columbia, Maryland 21045
(301) 730-2397

Editorial Offices
Suite 200-C
2901 Druid Park Drive
Baltimore, Maryland 21215

ISBN 0-935132-17-1
Library of Congress Card Catalog Number 89-081167
Manufactured in the United States of America
Second Printing: October, 1991

Dedication/Acknowledgements

This work is dedicated to the many people who made it possible. To my wife, Joy, and our children, Cara and David, who allowed me to write while abdicating household chores. To my mother, Margaret, who taught me, without knowing it, the real meaning of the Overcome.

To St. Katherine of Alexandria Episcopal Church and its members who suffered through the development of the concept with countless sermons on the issue, and who often misunderstood the content and its very intent. Many thought it was an appeal to material overcoming. Some still cannot understand that the only overcome that has value is conceptual and spiritual. It takes one "over" when all else is withdrawn.

Very special thanks go to my teacher and mentor, Professor Paul L. Holmer of Yale Divinity School. He taught me how concepts function within a language. The convincing analogy about "icy roads" communicating more than a description and carrying heavy imperatives came off his lips and rested on my mind so that in turn I could make the move from the introduction of the Overcome concept to the imperative to lead lives in the Overcome mood.

Professor Holmer influenced me greatly, and I truly thank him as I dedicate this book to one who was considered racist by fellow black students at Yale Divinity School in the early 1970's.

I also thank my publisher, Paul Evans, for his help throughout every editorial stage of this project.

Contents

Chapter One
The Need for a Black Overcome/Passover — 1

Chapter Two
Black Liberation Thinking: What It Does — 23

Chapter Three
Claim the Ghetto and Build Life-Saving Institutions — 39

Chapter Four
Black Liberation: More Than Consciousness-Raising — 61

Chapter Five
Dr. King's Death And Elevation:
The Symbol of the Overcome — 83

Chapter Six
The Overcome Unites All Blacks:
Christians, Muslims And
Rastafarians — 103

Chapter Seven
Concept Analysis:
Key to Black Liberation Thinking — 121

Chapter Eight
Liberation Is a Capacity Concept — 141

Chapter Nine
Language, Form of Life And Black Conventions — 159

Chapter Ten
Some Concluding Remarks — 185

Appendices — 191

Preface

Twenty-one years have now passed since the Civil Rights Movement was consummated in the death (sacrifice) of Dr. Martin Luther King, Jr. Dr. King was concerned about this question: "Where do we go from here?" He addressed that issue in economic and political terms in 1967. This book is also concerned about that very question. Where do we go from here? But its answer is different, in the first instant.

I believe that the first move out of the "crossroads" or dilemma that is suggested by this question about direction must be essentially conceptual. For there is no lack of programs, activities or even money in the black communities of America. We have enough of those. The lack resides elsewhere and the solution, as this book will indicate, is rather simple. But, it does not reside in programs, economics or things material. It is a "conceptual" solution that is needed and that will be offered in this book.

This book is not written to become one among many others that treat black problems, but it is written with the intent that it will serve to change the character and stature of blacks the world over. It seeks to change character, not by changing the name blacks are called or call each other one more time, but by simply adding to the repertoire of black thinking certain essential concepts that are missing—concepts about triumph, winning—the Overcome.

Some would immediately think that this book is simply playing with words. Wrong. One cannot think without concepts. Concepts are more than words alone. They carry descriptions, prescriptions, imperatives, conditions, etc. with them, whether spoken or not.

For example, to tell someone you love that the "roads outside are icy" gives more than a simple description. There is a silent imperative, a command if you will, to be careful in walking or driving. And anyone who understands the true meaning of icy roads would immediately pick up the hidden imperative. In like manner, when through this book I declare the Overcome for blacks

THE OVERCOME

worldwide, I am not simply changing the lyrics of a good and popular hymn or song: "We Shall Overcome." We are preparing the way for blacks to learn to think in the Overcome mood. We are offering a brand-new concept, the chief value of which is not to point to or describe any happening. Although it does that too.

The value is one of offering a new description of the character of the black man. He came from Africa, under very shameful conditions. He overcame the middle passage. He overcame the horrors of slavery. He overcame the setbacks of being free, yet considered three-fifths of a man for political purposes. And now, Martin Luther King, Jr. has been elevated to a status equal to George Washington and Abraham Lincoln, overcoming second-class status.

Many overcame their dislike for their color when in the sixties they turned the conceptual tables on those who cursed them with their color by saying, "Sing it loud, I'm black and I'm proud." They overcame so many negatives that were placed in their way: legal, systematic and otherwise that the black man and woman now emerging deserves a new persona, a new concept to describe not their color or the place of their origin, but the "content of their character."

After we establish the Overcome, a black Passover, the character of the black man and woman will change forever. They will now be known as men and women who overcome whatever is negative in their lives or community. The Overcome then becomes a character trait. It is not about money (in the first instance, it will be consequently), but about black propensities, predispositions, tendencies, habits and character. All the missing victory sub-concepts relevant to the black man must now be plugged into the matrix of the super-concept of the Overcome.

The black preacher and other leading change agents will need to offer saving content to the the black Overcome, ideas that are already present in the community, but which cannot take root until they are incorporated in the shared value of the society. The Overcome will "collect and hold," will interpret and pass on the successes, winnings, triumphs, victories, large and small of the community. The Overcome, which must be celebrated yearly, on April 4 (around Passover and Easter on the day our primary martyr was sacrificed), will guarantee that as other more creative minds get to work on this redeeming concept of the Overcome.

The Overcome then becomes the leading teaching tool for our children. Trouble, pain, poverty and pathology may be currently a part of the fabric of ghetto life. But, since others in worse times have overcome more (the middle passage and slavery), and since it is our nature to overcome, for we celebrate our societal overcome each year, then we overcome whatever is placed in our way. What a teaching tool! This is essentially what the Overcome, a black Passover, is all about.

"In the world you will have tribulations, but be of good cheer, I have overcome the world," Jesus said in John 16:33. The rest of the book is about demonstrating from many angles, using various examples, the need for the Overcome.

Who is the audience my publisher asked? All black people and all "under people." All who feel "under" by present circumstances are the potential audience. All who care about these things are urged to read through the pages of this book and discover the simplicity, power and value of introducing a victory concept like the Overcome to name victories, to guide, to sustain and reassure along the pilgrim's way.

In all you do, remember that the acceptance of the Overcome does not mean that it is time for complacency. There is a "done deal" aspect to the declaring of the Overcome. But, it functions more like the events around the purchasing of your first house with a 30-year mortgage. The house is yours and it is not. You have a generation, 30 years, in which to make that house yours. And just as the walk of 1,000 miles begins with that first step, so too does the purchasing of a house actually begins with the down payment, settlement and signing of a mortgage and promissory note.

The black Overcome like the Jewish Passover marks the beginning (not the end) of a victorious walk into the future.

Chapter One

The Need for a Black Overcome/Passover

This book has consumed my thoughts for over twenty years. However, it was a member of my congregation, Mrs. Carolyn Dungee, a woman of devout faith with no college degree or presumptions, who inspired me to finally do this work.

Several years ago, Mrs. Dungee asked me to introduce the Christian Seder supper at the church as part of the Holy Week Maundy Thursday rites.

I did not at that time even have an idea as to what seder was all about, and as a matter of fact I could not even spell the word. For two years I advertised it in the church bulletin as "sader," until Mrs. Dungee corrected me.

In this Christian Seder rite, I was always the father. The rite goes like this:[1]

> COMMENTATOR: At this season, the Jewish people celebrate the feast of the Passover, which commemorates their deliverance from slavery in Egypt. Jesus was a Jew, and today we wish to discover something of His life with His disciples by sharing a meal in a traditional Jewish style.
>
> ALL STAND. THE MOTHER LIGHTS THE CANDLES.
>
> MOTHER: Blessed are you, O Lord our God, King of the Universe, who has sanctified us by your commandments and commanded us to kindle the festival lights. Blessed are you, O Lord our God, King of the Universe, who has kept us alive and sustained us and brought us to this season. May our home be consecrated, O God, by the light of your face, shining on us in blessing and bringing us peace.
>
> ALL: Amen.

THE OVERCOME

ALL SIT. THE FATHER TAKES THE CUP OF WINE.

FATHER: Blessed are you, O Lord our God, King of the Universe, creator of the fruit of the vine. Blessed are you, O Lord our God, King of the Universe, who has chosen us among all peoples and sanctified us with your commandments. In love you have given us, O Lord our God, solemn days of joy and festive seasons of gladness, even this day of the feast of the unleavened bread, a holy assembly, a memorial of the departure from Egypt. Blessed are you, O Lord our God, who has preserved us, sustained us, and brought us to this season.

THE WINE IS POURED. ALL DRINK THE WINE.

COMMENTATOR: Now the Passover Story is retold. The youngest child asks the four traditional questions.

CHILD: Why is this night different from all other nights?

FATHER: In every generation, a man must so regard himself as if he came forth himself out of Egypt. God brought us out of bondage to freedom, from sorrow to gladness, and from darkness to great light.

CHILD: Why do we eat bitter herbs tonight at this special meal?

FATHER: Our fathers were slaves in Egypt, and their lives were made bitter. Our Lord tasted bitterness in His passion and death.

CHILD: Why do we eat lamb tonight at this special meal?

FATHER: At the time of the liberation from Egypt, God commanded each family to take a lamb, sacrifice it, eat it, and sprinkle its blood on the doorpost and lintel. And on that night, seeing the blood, the angel of the Lord passed over them and spared them. Christ is our lamb who sacrificed himself for us to give us eternal life with God.

CHILD: Why do we eat unleavened bread tonight at this special meal?

FATHER: When Pharaoh let our forefathers go from Egypt, they were forced to flee in great haste. They had no time to bake their bread; they could not wait for the yeast to rise. The sun baked it into flat unleavened bread.

COMMENTATOR: In thanksgiving for liberation, we say a psalm of praise:

ALL: Praise the Lord all you nations. Praise him all you peoples. His constant love for us is strong, and His faithfulness is eternal. Praise the Lord.

THE MATZO IS BROKEN BY THE FATHER AND DISTRIBUTED.

ALL: Blessed are you, O Lord our God, King of the Universe, who brings forth bread from the earth.

THE MATZO IS EATEN AND THEN THE BITTER HERB IS DISTRIBUTED.

ALL: Blessed are you, O Lord our God, King of the Universe, who has sanctified us by your commandments and commanded us concerning the eating of bitter herbs.

THE BITTER HERB IS EATEN, AND THE LAMB IS DISTRIBUTED.

ALL: Blessed are you, O Lord God, King of the Universe, who delivered us from bondage and saved us in the blood of the lamb.

THE LAMB IS EATEN, THEN ALL EAT SUPPER.

FATHER: The Lord bless you and keep you. The Lord make His face to

A BLACK PASSOVER

shine upon you and have mercy on you and give you peace.
ALL SING THE DOXOLOGY.

This seder rite, obviously a modification of the Jewish rite, forced on me questions about meaning, purposing and placing in the scheme of life. I found myself answering with great effect, but more like an actor than one actually participating in the shared recall of a salvation event. I answered the young child from another's set of historical experiences and myths and not from my own.

The contemplation of this reminded me of an experience at Codrington College in Barbados back in 1968. This was after learning of Dr. Martin Luther King's death, and after Andrew Young, the former ambassador to the United Nations and the former mayor of Atlanta, visited us there for a recovery break from the traumatic experience of having lost his friend and leader. I was called a heretic by fellow students and faculty for simply suggesting then that there was a striking similarity between Dr. King and Jesus, who as Christ, is seen as Christians' sacrificial Passover.

For years I could do nothing with this theme in my head. Professor William R. Jones, who taught me at the Yale Divinity School, in his book, *Is God A White Racist?*,[2] further confounded the notion when he declared that no person in black history could function as the redemptive suffering servant. Joseph Washington had written that blacks are God's contemporary suffering servants. But, Professor Jones would show that such a claim could not stand apart from blacks also identifying the exalting/validating event. In other words, apart from identifying this exalting/validating event, the vicarious suffering servant model could not be effectively used by blacks at this time.

Then came Representative Parren J. Mitchell (D., Md.), then a member of Congress and a member of my congregation, who along with other black congressmen, spearheaded the passage of the bill making Dr. King's birthday a national holiday. And now, we finally had one who was "downed"; one who suffered innocently for his people, being raised up, and elevated for us. In that landmark event, the description of Dr. King's death as "assassination" radically changed to a new description, that of "sacrifice." The change is validated by him being

THE OVERCOME

lifted up. And now, the work, written by one who has been now out of academia for almost twelve years, had to be done. At least, it could trigger the interest of the better, more formal academic minds and serve to get things going in the "Overcome key." If this is accomplished; if the great preachers, teachers and change agents in the black community can overlook the weaknesses and get to the essence and identify the strategic relevance of this work, then something good will no doubt result.

I came from an island background that once experienced slavery. There, something of an Overcome/Passover rite is done annually on the first of August. I am certain that something similar is needed if we are to get a handle on black pathology, overcoming it in order to get to the building and instituting stage and age. Moreover, the analogy, and that is all that it is, between the Jewish Passover, and what we shall call the "Black Overcome," was insightfully made in 1834 by Harriet Martineau, who accounted for the events that took place in Antigua, West Indies on August 1, 1834 in the following way:[3]

> The first of August fell on a Friday, and there was to be a holiday from Thursday night until Monday. The missionaries did their duty well, and completely succeeded in impressing the people with a sense of the solemnity of the occasion. It was to the Negroes their Passover night. They were all collected in their chapels—the Wesleyans keeping watch night in the chapels throughout the island. The pastors recommended to the people to receive the blessing in silence and on their knees. At the first stroke of midnight from the great cathedral bell, all fell on their knees, and nothing was heard but the slow tolling bell and some struggling sobs in the intervals. The silence lasted for a few moments after the final strokes, when a peal of awful thunder rattled through the sky, and the flash of lightening seemed to put out the lamps in the chapels. Then the kneeling crowd sprang to their feet and gave voice to their passionate emotions—such voice as might be expected from this excitable people. Some tossed up their free arms and groaned away at once the heart's burden of life. Families and neighbors opened their hearts to each other. Some prayed aloud, after the lead of their pastors, that they might be free indeed; and a voice was heard in thanksgiving for a

real Sabbath now, when the wicked should cease from troubling, and the weary be at rest, and the voice of the oppressor should be no more heard, and the servant should be free from his master. In some of the chapels the noble spectacle was seen, of masters attending with their Negroes, and when the clock had struck, shaking hands with them, and wishing them joy. The rest of the holiday was spent partly in mirth, as was right, and much of it in listening to the addresses of the missionaries, who urged them, with much force, and in the utmost detail, the duties of sobriety and diligence, and harmony with their employers. On Monday morning they went to work—work that they were proud of now, as it was for wages.

Martineau likened the event "to the Negroes' Passover night," and if Jews were indeed once slaves in Egypt, trapped in the oppressive situation and found their way out via the Passover events, then the analogy takes on real potency and could be made to mean and function for blacks. And, I call us all to examine it with me for pointers to a redemptive way out.

I hope that as you read and think with me, the words will capture your imagination, and somehow transform the way you look at the black situation in America and the larger world. I bring a rather presumptuous intention with me to this work, but I hardly apologize for it. For there is that sense in which the title of a book, *Poor, Black and in Real Trouble*,[4] written by a native Baltimorean, Jerome Dyson-Wright, captures the black situation. There is little doubt that for many such a phrase adequately describes the current situation. Now twenty years after Dr. King's life, ministry and sacrificial death, and three years after the ultimate black martyr's vindication, elevation and exaltation, it is time for the work to begin in earnest. The interpretive work that will guarantee that his living, his sacrificial dying and his consequent elevation, will not be in vain and without instructive, reconstructive and redemptive significance.

My argument is that blacks, who to date have not yet capitalized on the redemptive significance of the life, work, death and vindicating elevation of Dr. King, must begin now to re-think their lineal view of history—seen as an endless pilgrimage, always walking but never arriving—and discover that there is no "saving" or overcoming possible from this way of thinking. My arguments will challenge us to look again, and point to the need to examine dogmatic theology, prescriptive philosophy, religion, psychology, education and language for "Overcome" models. Using the Jewish Passover myth as an operational paradigm, I shall argue from all angles the need, no, rather the requirement, for making Dr. King's life/sacrificial death/elevation event serve as the before/after interpretive historical happening that will set the stage for the introduction of a new beginning self-description of blacks—something I believe must happen before true peoplehood can be established.

I hope by the end of this book to lead to a conclusion that much as the Jews did their Passover in story and rite prior to their leaving slavery in Egypt, so blacks must now do their Overcoming/Passover through the blood of Dr. King, and establish once and for all that needed interpretive "break" with the past way of seeing and doing, of hoping and intending, and of wishing and singing. This is the break between under/over human status, and move forward into the future, thinking, singing, talking and doing in an "over" rather than an "under" mood and mode.

Blacks are, without doubt, trapped. I happen to believe that the entrapment is transfield—linguistic, conceptual, cultural, religious, historical, psychological and economic. In other words, it is complete. As an example, blacks cannot yet establish the name by which they will be called or will call themselves.

There is indeed conceptual and linguistic trouble when, at the core, a race cannot establish its name. Our names have included nigger, colored and Negro. Then, during the Black Power Movement, we were called black, and supposedly proudly so. But, only for a time. For now, Afro-American is the name with some, and African-American is again becoming popular with others. We are always a minority, even in Democratic cities in which we are numerical majorities. Who are we? And, can we ever move forward before we discover our name?

A name establishes character. It bears individual and corporate history. But whose history will it be when written? Black peoples' that could include all blacks, whatever their origin? Or, exclusive of the newcomers from the Pacific Islands and even from Mother Africa, as we talk only about the Afro/African-American? I would counsel that we watch the names that we call each other and by which we are called and that we establish our name. I counsel such as I ask an honest answer about what you think about a person who changes his name not once for meaning, but six times in 20 years?

So, we are conceptually and linguistically trapped. We all know how we are economically, psychologically and racially trapped.

In what I am attempting to do, I will offer you no new knowledge about anything. I am not seeking to offer another opinion, another truth or develop any new truths about reality. If you were to inquire about my motives, I would simply declare that blacks are trapped in a conceptual prison (bondage). We know it, are desperate to find a way out, and have tried just about everything so far, except concept analysis.

We have tried the vocational educational programs of Booker T. Washington;[5] the legal persuasion of the NAACP; the programming of the Urban League; the migrationism of Marcus Garvey; the moral/ethical persuasion of Dr. King; the political activism of Jesse Jackson; the economic empowerment of Parren J. Mitchell; the separation into nation within nation of Malcolm X and the Muslims; and yet the ultimate description about being poor, black and in real trouble continues.

Even though some major progress has been made, we are still generally described as being on the fringes of American society, as we remain politically, socially, economically, culturally and conceptually trapped.

"The situation of the black man in America is desperate and baffling. Our situation is radical and unique and complicated. It requires new strategies, new programs, new philosophies and new interpreters. It requires a new orientation of the black man's thinking (conceptual) about the society in which he lives and about himself,"[6] says Bishop Joseph A. Johnson. Such statements assure me of the need for the black Overcome/Passover.

The above quotation gets us quickly to the point at which I could declare and proclaim that all black thinking, writing, talking, hoping, intending, trying, theologizing about the black situation to date has been and is being done from a pre-liberation standpoint. Everything still must be accomplished. There are no "done victory deals," and because there is very little to be lifted up, the songs remain dirge-like[7] and nothing really or essentially changes.

The clear call is for a new way of seeing, intending, hoping and doing in the world of black experience. The recognition is there of the many failed programs, the many tried and failed approaches. The ongoing scenario is one in which it is fashionable to invent something new, try it, fail at it, and file it as another failure. And so, we discover that what is being filed, what is overwhelmingly imprinted on the corporate mind, is not a series of successes, but of failures. And, because there are few identifiable Overcome/done deals, there is not much that could form the basis for instituting the paradigm success story that will in turn become the foundation for effective change. That which I seek to offer here could also join the long tradition of attempts at coming up with something else. I am proposing that blacks use the life, ministry, sacrificial death and elevation (which functions like resurrection) of Dr. King as our Overcome/Passover happening, a means for gaining the teaching handle needed in interpreting our story—the means for starting again from a dated beginning.

Presumptuous? Perhaps. Who authorizes this? Who granted permission? I will answer that the logic and grammar of the black man's plight; the logical geography of his total pathological situation, as described by him, requires that we move from the wrong side of Overcome/Passover, where we seek permission, and move over to the other side (the Overcome flip) where we assume the responsibility for our total futures.

In succeeding chapters, I will point to the pattern that has emerged whereby Martin Luther King, Jr. is identified as a type of Moses, the liberator. Dr. King's going to the "mountaintop" might have triggered this identification. I will again pick up on this theme and do an analysis of the type of freedom and liberation Moses actually designed for the children of Israel, comparing it with Dr. King and in that exercise demonstrate once more our own need for declaring, proclaiming, celebrating and instituting our Overcome/Passover happening through Dr. King, and thereafter follow the footsteps of Moses and the redeemed children of Israel. This means to walk prosperously into the future building moral codes, rites of passage, covenants and life-saving and supporting institutions that can in time create for blacks the true connectedness as a people, one to the other, wherever we may find ourselves in the world, and whatever be the current existential situation, dominant religion, or political happenings. Unlike the call from Marcus Garvey to return to Africa, the retort is a different one. The challenge is to "claim the ghetto" or wherever you now are. Make it, at least at the first stage, your very own promised land.

<u>This</u> <u>must</u> come first, and with a God-given-like quality-like myth not being up for question at this beginning genesis level. We are to use it as source for our answers to our children about the meaning of black life and experience, and it is strategically placed to serve to focus our unity and resolve.

The Jewish Passover event captures for us the importance of establishing that story which begins the re-interpretation of our salvation history, with our salvation being already won at some level through the efforts and blood of one of our own people, with the help of our God.

It will be shown that there is a sense in which the experience of blacks of the African diaspora and the Jews who were slaves in Egypt meets and touches across time and space. Both peoples were held for about the same number of years—400 years according to Exodus and history. They were held long enough to lose their identity, their culture and language. The men were effectively taken out of the picture in both accounts, in one case by infanticide and in the other by incarceration, joblessness and the development of a matriarchy in the black culture.

When Moses opted to confront the Pharaoh regarding the freedom of his people, he initially did exactly what Dr. King did. He went asking permission to go. "Let my people go," he pleaded. On receiving the resounding "No!," each time he would do a demonstration of resolve. The similarity here with Dr. King is astounding. Moses delivered plagues and Dr. King rousing speeches and record-setting peace marches and demonstrations of resolve. But, it is here that the similarities end.

For Moses, after 10 pleadings and correlated demonstrations (plagues), activities with beginnings and

THE OVERCOME

endings that did not work, resolved never to return to the Pharaoh. He would never again ask permission. He stopped the begging, reasoning and debating and instead returned to his people to create and establish the Passover ceremony of spilled blood, of accomplishment, of resolve, the ceremony of the done deal, of the "never again this humiliation theme," and with and through that simple Passover/bridge/flick/flip event, that one simple activity in the salvation history of the Jews, the slaves became former slaves, garnered the inner strength they always had but never felt confident enough to use, and they walked. As they walked, they were prepared to make their own gods, first from silver and gold, the act through which they sought to break their ties with the value system of the oppressors they were now leaving behind.

Through their Passover event, they at once established and installed for all time the communal, corporate victory, which would forever and always mark the break, the before/after of "under slave days" and after "overpassed days." A little reflection will remind us that they did this while they were yet slaves and not over 100 years later. They left with a certain resolve to overcome as they had already done in Egypt any and every obstacle to their fully achieving their vision of a promised land, filled with milk and honey, or all things good and necessary for their well-being as a people. These would prove to be many for a truly primitive band of people, who as yet had no political system, no economic power, no worthwhile institutions at this level, but one, a young Passover, days old, that would serve as the communal, corporate victory, especially in times when things were not going well. They began their liberation walk with a "manufactured" victory.

There would be future rivalry for power. There were many testings of the god, the making of many others. The Israelites would debate different ways of going about things, to be inclusive or exclusive (to integrate or not in common parlance). But, they always remained connected in and through the Passover happening. The history of the Israelites would detail that it saw them through many and varied vicissitudes and perplexities. In our day, it carried the Jewish people through the Holocaust. But somehow, that first Passover, a concoction by Moses for strategic reasons, has become that which holds the Jews together across Diaspora, language barriers, cultures, time and space. Each succeeding age could look back and gain strength to go on overcoming or passing-over perplexities. As a black man informed by a culture without a unifying passover, I wonder just how a Jew could dare to celebrate and "do" Passover during the Holocaust in such an existentially powerless situation, without hope, and ripe for despair. Yet many "did" Passover. Blacks who contemplate these things must see the redemptive necessity for the black Overcoming/Passover as preliminary to our moving from the pre-liberative status, in which we are now stuck, to the liberation status we all seek. For one thing, it establishes the separation of eras (before/after) that is absolutely necessary, if we are to go on.

Our black liberation thinkers who have sought paradigms of liberation have for the most part skirted over the key element of liberation, even when examining Moses and his liberating efforts. That missed element is all that is currently lacking in the completion of the first stage of liberation. For if we are ever to move from the pre-liberation stance to true liberation status, we must also identify, declare, proclaim, celebrate our overcoming Passover. It must be popularly accepted, and duly incorporated into the corpus of conventions that guide and govern black lives. An appropriate ceremony, with the same symbols and words must be devised, and a means of initiating people into the Overcome experience (for Jews it is circumcision) must be developed. So, all who wish to participate in the Overcome experience would be duly initiated and charged regarding the requirements for entering and the responsibilities for building the life-saving and supporting institutions that will hold them in the Overcome state.

For blacks, I will dare to suggest that the simple changing of the lyrics of their chief pre-liberation hymn could indeed signal the advent of the Overcome. We will need to change "We Shall Overcome Someday" to "We Have Overcome Today."

I have already alluded to the fact that the introduction of the Passover model of liberation as applicable to blacks is by no means new. It was done in the West Indies in 1834. And as suggested above, it has become dominant as many continue to see Dr. King as the black Moses. The problem is that the Moses that Dr. King is identified with is the pre-liberation Moses. The one who begs, persuades and demonstrates. This Moses, like Dr. King before his sacrifice and elevation, was "activity defined." The speeches, the demonstrations, the marches, the plagues were all activity related. Activities always have beginnings, middles and endings. They can be stopped and started again. Moses, an "activity defined man" at the pre-liberation stage, found himself up against a "dispositionally defined man" in the person of the Pharaoh, a man certain of his status and standing, knowing where he came from, where he now stood, and where he was going.

In any attempt to match an activity defined man over against a dispositionally defined man, the former will come out the loser. In order to demonstrate this key difference between Moses of the pre-liberation era and the Pharaoh and Moses of the post-Passover era, we shall need to look at language, and through this discover the key differences between liberation and liberators functioning first via activities and those who function from the dispositional stance. This is how concept analysis will get applied in the later chapters of this work.

And it will be through this process that we discover that liberation is essentially a dispositional, character, achievement word and never in essence of the nature of the strivings, battles and stages. So many seem to think that liberation (Overcome) points to the many tryings in process and not to the accomplishment after the process of trying has yielded some victories.

In the Jewish liberation model, we find most of what we need: under-status as slaves; at the right time, the liberator arises; makes his various pitches; and does his myriads of demonstrations, acts, speeches. Always the same response of ambivalence—yes/no or resolute no. Then, the under person (Moses in this case) is himself transformed, and he becomes a man of equal resolution and stature. He "shakas"[8]—stands tall—and changes his way of looking at the situation from the vantage point of his new status. He "overcomes" in approach and tailors his intendings, hopings and doings in the Overcome mood and mode. He still has many of the same things to do, but

A BLACK PASSOVER

he now does them in the Overcome mood and mode. And he wins. So far, blacks have fallen short of the one thing necessary for overcoming at the first stage. They refuse to make the "flip"; that is, the conceptual flip from "under" to "over." This flip must take place whether it comes gradually or in a flash, as students sometimes suddenly learn (capacity) after teachers have been teaching (activity). But when they learn, the moves are essentially different. The moves are theirs as teachers of themselves and others. They can continue the series and make essentially new moves and combinations of moves that no one had taught them before.

Overcome/Passover will function for blacks essentially as the corporate success/achievement concept in the black community. There, individuals are already busy doing the Overcome flip after discovering their plight and the inner capabilities to do the individual Overcome/Passover bridging thing. Individual lives are being changed, and such individuals, be they Mohammed Ali or Reginald Lewis, change their lives, find a way (hard or easy) and go on to stack victories. But again, in the black community, there are virtually no corporate success words. In later chapters, we shall look at just how success words function. Here we will simply state that a form of life, any form of life, is dependent upon the quality of human consciousness; that is, ways of caring in the world with many possibilities for winning and losing. Man always does his caring, intending and hoping within the framework of the form of life that frames him, limits and qualifies him. And herein lies another of my great fears for my people, black people, which could only be effectively remedied by the introduction of the Overcome/Passover.

For with a language and dominant form of life (same as culture) that has few if any victory stories, myths, historical instances of overcoming; that is, winning through heroes, real or in story books, one should not wonder at the abundant manifestation of negatives on the conceptual, linguistic and behavioral levels. For as we think, so we sing, write poetry, walk and live. And the truly frightening aspect of this situation is our knowing that both the "form of life followed" and the language spoken, limit and qualify and in the case of blacks, entrap.

We shall need, I suspect, to boldly install into the

THE OVERCOME

language and form of life of blacks some key victory concepts. If they are not actually there and resident in the culture and history—the corporate memory—then aspects of the history and corporate memory must be redone in such a way as to create identifiable moments of victory, identifiable heroes, and easy to tell and recall stories about how they "overcame" and expect us in our day and time to do the same. And, after recognizing that individuals have overcome, the culture, the body corporate of blacks, must together install the event/moment through which all declare "a participatory victory" over the forces that serve as stoppers. There is a need to install in the language and culture the concept of Overcome/Passover as prerequisite for empowering the language and form of life to "speak and do" in the Overcome mood and mode.

The concepts of a language are that through which the culture communicates; the means whereby lives are shaped and formed. It should be obvious that certain aspects of liberation remain absent from the language and form of life with no concepts of victory, triumph, celebration or accomplishment that is not individual and therefore can be shared or participated in. And, with no myths or heroes, no King David who kills 10,000, no King Arthur and his Round Table, no Fourth of July or Waterloo, and no Passover, no wonder that blacks remain conceptually trapped. The initial work has not yet been done. I am persuaded that the event (and many supporting happenings) is already in the culture. We have the ready-made moment. The MLK story can easily be made, but we have not yet found a way to corporately turn this God-given happening in our day and time into the Overcoming black Passover flip-event. This happens by installing it in the language and form of life so that it can in due time form and govern lives, as our children feed on it, as the culture takes on the massive task of nurturing the capabilities, propensities, and abilities that must accompany the introduction of the "Overcome concept."

For its installation and inculcation are that which will in the end and in due turn make possible—that is, permit—our people to look at the world, think, do and institute in the world in the Overcome way. My strategic concerns have to do with how "over" lives are formed. And, I know that in any key area in which an ingredient necessary for the Overcome life is missing from the body of informative conventions and from the language that holds those conventions, then we must first install them. And, the installation of the corporate black Overcome/Passover is the surest way I know to go about this valued task of installing a new victory concept that would function for the whole community of blacks.

The introduction of new concepts is easy for men and women of status and power like Winston Churchill or Lyndon Johnson. It is not easy when it is a small town priest who gets this daring. A long treatise is needed. Yet, it must be done.

In the end, it will not be good only for the blacks either. For whites in their right minds already know that blacks must quickly get to the point at which they not only take charge of their futures, but they must begin to make larger contributions to the society. Whites know that a minority population that is growing as fast as blacks cannot forever and always remain one in which 90 percent are truly "under," depending on the largess of the white community or depending on the 10 percent of their number who are doing well, but hiding their successes from their brothers for some good and very bad reasons.

The "Overcome" way of seeing and doing for blacks will require the development of capabilities that will make the above pointers possible. This comes, I will show, through the mastery of the concepts with their prescriptive, indicative and imperative aspects all intact. The one lingering danger in the entire process is the fact that some of these key concepts have not yet been installed in the culture and its language. They must be installed before the first liberative steps can be taken. And so, those who wonder with the preachers and other leading change agents why after 20 years so little progress has been made, would better think on these things, as they look again not for any radically new facts, but with a new perspective on viewing and managing the extant facts. Discover why it is absolutely necessary for us to first install victory, Overcome and triumphalism as done deals that are somehow repeatable by ordinary folk. They are repeatable because ordinary folk, black folk, in more troubled times than these, found a way to come out winners. They went to mountaintops and from there saw

THE OVERCOME

all things differently.

That we have not yet done this is only another sign of our pre-liberation status. We may indeed be feeling that we actually have no authority to do this daring thing. But, I will always demand that we give ourselves this authority to install these liberating notions, the ones that would be needed to serve as success criteria. This is so that in turn these liberating notions can be used as a source, to inform, govern and even shame us if in the "after Overcome time" our language and our behavior/actions do not match that new positive imagery the Overcome language and form or life will force upon us.

We will be led in subsequent chapters to see that although such successes or achievement words and concepts may resemble activity words that they are actually different in their grammar and core. We will show that task words predicate the activities involved in given performances. We will show that a task verb is very much like the kicking of the soccer ball and that achievement words or concepts are those which record the scoring of a goal or point.

When in due time we are led to understand that achievement concepts must be seen as those that crown the activities pointed to by the task/activity words, then we shall understand that task verbs point to the tryings, the processes. Achievement words register the satisfactory (by convention, by judgment of the umpire, referee or critical audience) completion of the task. In a very real sense, therefore, achievement words will not chiefly belong on the lips or in the mouth of the player, learner or actor, but more so on the lips of the umpire, teacher, evaluator and audience. For achievement words— and Overcome is one such word—are not used to describe the many tryings in process, but the things gained, acquired or mastered after the many trials. Hence, we might claim that success implies that one has overcome the obstacles in the way by victorious attempts at turning the "I can't do that feeling" into the "I can do that, and I have already done that. Or, one just like me, in worse times, has successfully done that, and grants me the participatory permission to claim it as my own victory."

A laborious attempt to explain the crucially significant difference between activity/task verbs and dispositional/capacity/achievement/mastery words will be strategically key to our understanding the arguments put forth in this book where we claim that liberty, like "passover" and "overcome," is of the nature of capacity/mastery word concepts.

We will be making the fatally dysfunctional error if we continue to make category mistakes in this critical flip-over area. For such is the type of category mistakes that trap us into continually stringing one episode, one demonstration, one program after another in endless sequence. And, all the time being very busy indeed, peddling, but never actually achieving, arriving, gaining mastery, overcoming or passing over—always and forever on the way, but never arriving.

Our call is one that gets blacks to see that after the Overcome happening, we shall continue to do everything we have done before and perhaps many other activities we have not yet tried. We may even need to march, demonstrate, and plan programs, along with other activities that have to do with building institutions. But, we will do them in a different mood, from a different stance and vantage point.

I have personally found this distinction, located as it is in the area of the conceptual leap/flip from "task verb" to "dispositional notion," where we make things our own, part of the repertoire of our competencies, where we are transformed from the drudgery of instruction to the mastery of learning, where we move from under status to over status, quite instructive in considering black liberation issues. Black thinkers and preachers and change agents are perhaps missing this key distinction between "try verbs" and "got it" nouns. And so, we all go on, and forever pleading, blaming, crying, singing, describing pathological problems, but never claiming any major victory—real or mythologically contrived—that give reason for pause and recall and celebration, for rest breaks between more periods of trying and more moments of succeeding. I suspect that we need at least one big mythological victory through which corporate Overcoming for blacks can be celebrated. This must come first, so it can give meaning and pause and hope and reason for believing that more victories lie ahead.

I say this because I know that in the placing of the

beginning myth, it cannot be "failure specific." It must be "success specific." The story that will get us going must also at some stage take on the character of myth, a larger than life victory story through which the transcending aspects of the Overcome are located. It must be about achievement and success, and it must be a done deal, one that need never be done again. And, even if in the placing of the myth, the work is initially clumsily done and knotted at the tie like a balloon (our systems balloon)[9], it must still be done and now. It will have beginning systems problems. Perhaps there will be problems like those to be found in the creation story in Genesis with Adam's mothering of Eve at least in the beginning: the Passover lamb's blood being actually efficacious and the Virgin Birth and Jesus' Resurrection.

Such events cannot be seen as up for question. They further serve, rather, as beginning theorems. And the Overcome, by nature, cannot be either seen as one other idea or opinion among others. Such can never be effective as one man's opinion or as another party issue or "ism." Why? If the Overcome will function correctly, it is itself to be used as the interpreter of all the "isms" in the community. At this basic level, taking party sides will not be permissible.

For there is no room for party issues and "isms" at this basic, foundational, genesis level. For the issues important to parties, their "isms," are never foundational, since each depends upon the weakness or incorrectness of the other. At this most basic level, division cannot be made a part of the foundational logic in the redemptive process. Party issues are being developed in the black community: Dr. King and his Vision Glorious of the beloved integrated community that is so closely related to the NAACP persuasion philosophy, but very different indeed from Marcus Garvey's migrationism and Malcolm X's nation-building. Even the Urban League's programming can source a party logic and approach.

These, if allowed to happen, will seed divisiveness at the core because all "isms" and party issues are questionable and divisive, gaining their strength from the weaknesses detected in others. Rather, what I propose must find its locale in logic or grammar where (like theorems in mathematics, or tenets of religion, or articles of faith) they are true by definition. What I propose could also be located in myth with its ability to take away the historic negatives and elevate the communal positives. However, when located in myth, the parties involved must always be aware of the limits of myth, while recognizing its massive capability for conveying life-saving, community integrating and redeeming truth, all of a nature very different from historic or scientific truths, but better able to convey saving truth because it is freed from the limitations of time and space and peculiarity.

Finally, our call for changing the pre-liberation hymn, "We Shall Overcome Someday," to the liberation hymn, "We Have Overcome Today," reminds us of another conceptual problem. It embodies a lineal view of history and overcoming—process and activity-like at the core. Perhaps our total reliance on history rather on philosophy or dogmatic theology is serving us negatively at this point.

Our current reliance on history and facts on the one hand and scientific-like evidence on the other hand make us ask: Where is the evidence? I will also ask where was the evidence (scientific-like) for the Jews when they declared Passover? This was a primitive band of vagrant slaves daring to change (conceptually) the activity-based verb "to pass over" into the accomplishment resident noun, "Passover," making it name a done deal that presupposes accomplishment. Where was the scientific evidence?

There was miraculous evidence. But, to describe something as miracle runs counter to scientific evidence, being a function of theological add-ons. But, those primitive Jews knew the process well back then. They simply changed the process verb into the accomplishment noun, as Moses did Passover, thereby placing the first victory, a victory located in story, rite and ritual at the first stage, a beginning story, which places unquestionable success at the beginning of the Passover walk, with the help of God. Try dissecting the Passover. For that matter, try dissecting the other significant beginning stories in the Bible, like creation, Virgin Birth, Resurrection, and Pentecost.

Blacks place their Passover/Victory/Overcome in the future. The Jews did it first, conceptually, and in rite and ritual. They have spent the rest of their history proving that what began conceptually, and what at first could only be evidenced in rite and ritual, can in due time be evidenced in every other significant fashion. So, after changing the verb "to pass over" into a character resident noun, Passover, they equipped themselves to walk, hope and think differently. They became the "Passover people." Passover redescribed their corporate character. They went on to conquer and to build life-saving and life-sustaining institutions, institutions that would keep them going even in times when there would be no great charismatic leader or movement.

But, we continue to see things in lineal fashion, in progress and procession, with little being done even to define who it is that is on the pilgrimage, where he is going, and what will signal his arrival. The simple question has to do with this: What will serve as criteria for success? In other words, how will even the one in pilgrimage know that he has arrived? Our two or more picturings of the Vision Glorious will not help either. Malcolm X's "Nation Within Nation" and King's "Beloved Community," where all Americans stride forward integrated hand in hand, offer further cause for contradiction and conceptual confusion, apart from the introduction of the unifying story, the would-be source for both visions. In subsequent chapters, I will point to the Jewish people's way of handling both dreams as they live by a rule of "together and yet so far away."

The picture, be it in Pikesville, Maryland or Brooklyn, New York, is one for the Jews in which they separate in the community for political, religious, cultural and economic strength, and integrate themselves fully in the city, Wall Street, and commercial centers, in transcultural and philanthropic matters. They move in and out with great ease. The Jewish paradigm of living the "Passover life" across time and space, in good times and bad, surfaces again to offer redemptive pointers to black theologians, philosophers, preachers and other change agents.

It can, without doubt, offer the beginning logic and grammar for framing and governing the new visioning for blacks as they seek to function in the "Overcome" mood and mode.

A BLACK PASSOVER

Notes on Chapter One

[1] This is an adaptation of the Seder Rite for Christians. Its authorship is unknown. It was taken from a loose flier with no credits.

[2] William R. Jones, *Is God a White Racist?*, (Garden City, New York, Anchor Press/Doubleday, 1973).

[3] F. E. Peters. The Abolition of Slavery, (Barbados, W.I., Advocate Press, 1934), p. 12.

[4] Jerome Dyson-Wright, *Poor, Black And in Real Trouble*, Baltimore.

[5] Adaptation from the address of Bishop Joseph A. Johnson, May, 1970, in Gayraud S. Wilmore and James H. Cone, "Black Theology: A Documentary History, 1966-1979," (Maryknoll, New York, Orbis Books, 1979,) p. 281.

[6] Ibid, p. 281.

[7] Ibid, Paul Holmer, p. 189.

[8] "Shakas"—the name of an African King warrior who stood his ground against imperialists. As used here, it means "to take a stand, stand tall and live by the consequences of one's actions."

[9] I have concluded that all conceptual systems, even after they have been logically put together, must be secured by an ugly knot that holds it all together. I call this the "system balloon knot." It functions like a balloon, all round and smooth at the top, and good for holding the air. But there is always that ugly and problematic knot. The creation stories, the Exodus, the Resurrection are all fashioned in this way. They function to get things started, and scientific and analytic investigations are not appropriate. For such function as the beginning theorems to get the enterprise started. In a real sense, the black Overcome/Passover must fit this "systems balloon" mold as it is recognized that its strategic function is one of getting the black redemptive enterprise on its upward, futuristic, victorious and triumphant way. Our work must fall somewhere in this general area.

Chapter Two

Black Liberation Thinking: What It Does

I commend the pioneers in black theology and black liberation thinking for the descriptions they have developed about what black liberation theology is. The descriptions remain adequate.

These pioneers claim, quite correctly, that the existential absurdities that are manifested in the lives of black Americans require redemptive and liberative treatment by black theologians, philosophers and religionists whose chief work has to do with first making sense of racism and inequity and the apparent absurdities that are manifested in the lives of black Americans.

Most of these thinkers have chosen to do this in the light of the Christian story with its many beautiful themes and types—justice, love, brotherhood, liberality, etc.—in short, in light of its picture of the coming "Kingdom of God."

I do not only commend, but I also thank the pioneers in these areas for their bold and daring leadership in forcing the existential and pathological conditions of blacks into the theological arena, thereby widening the context of theology to include the forgotten, suffering minority, who were often treated with benign neglect, as if their condition required no consideration in God-talk.

That pathos, that absurdity, which refused to be fitted within the neat systems that managed concepts like the problem of evil and the peculiarity of ethnic suffering, was boldly addressed by the pioneering black theologians.

And, even though the exercise caused much pain, they stood their ground and started ripples that affected and transformed the neat theological systems that had to date placed the issues special and peculiar to black people on the extreme fringes to exist there as the "loose ends" that could not fit. The pioneering black theologians made them fit, no matter how clumsy the work now becomes.

And so, all theology must in a sense be done over to include treatment of blacks and to help frame the answer to the larger human question: "What has God to say about racism and its effect in America?" As one scholar loves to say, "What meaneth this?"

Consequently, I admit that I have no major problem with most of the descriptions of what black theology is, but I do find some difficulties and intellectual frustrations in considering a range of related issues about what black liberation theology "does." Is it serving the people well? Is it functional or dysfunctional and to what end?

Is its current starting point, rooted as it is in the pathological descriptions of black people, the years of slavery and since, instructive or enhancing? Is its limitation to the last 450 years in the history of black people, just in America, the years of slavery and the pre-liberation years since, instructive? Is its assertion that the Negro spirituals and the "blues" are the matrix for its development and consequent interpretation in its best vital interests? What is its picture of the Vision Glorious or what would count as success criteria in the so-called liberation struggle?

Moyd and Cone claim that in the spirituals and the blues, a form of religious music, can be located the matrix of black liberation theology. But, they are talking about a political theology or strategy. The early black preachers knew what they were doing with their specialized language of preaching and singing through spirituals. They were setting the stage for political redemption.

Religious redemption was already established through Jesus. But, political (existential) redemption was yet to be achieved.

The sad thing is that after the black preacher of ages past succeeded in saving the race of black people from certain genocide with their teaching—no wine, no woman, no song, no economic earthly ambitions to challenge the power of whites, even after using songs like "O' Canaan" to announce the Underground Railroad trip to Canada—in contemporary black preaching, all the black preachers have garnered from their historic teachers are the medium and style.

For the effective medium and style of the black preacher remains intact for the most part, but it is lacking of content appropriate to the end of saving an entire people. The pioneers in black preaching certainly had content appropriate for saving blacks from certain genocide in the days when the style of black preaching was being developed.

In a real sense, what many contemporary black preachers are doing, even the most successful of the lot, is sadly pathetic. They are for the most part inferior in quality to their forebears who knew what they were doing—saving the race. The modern black preacher often continues with the same medium, style and content of the black preacher of yesteryear with everything intact. But, they make one fundamental prophetic mistake of being fundamentalist where their forebears were being symbolic. So they literalize and fossilize that which ought to be prophetically symbolic.

It seems to me that much like the Jews created an interpretive matrix of mythology, mixed with history, to handle their liberation from slavery at the hands of black men in Egypt, so too must black liberation thinkers go beyond the 400 years of slavery to a more glorious time when blacks in Egypt were developing one civilization after another while Europe remained barbarous. The Jews went back and created interpretive stories about beginnings; mythologies about Abraham, Issac and Jacob. They claimed to have come from lofty beginnings, lost it for a while, that their God and good leaders will bring them promised foretold redemption and blessings. Then, they fashioned redemptive stories, rules and covenants between them and their God and between each other, covenants and rules that would not only hold them together as a people, but would become the corpus of conventions that would be forever used to "settle" all problems be they personal or other.

Most important of all, they manufactured and instituted for all time their Passover/liberation/overcoming, a once-for-all-time event that would in the future become the reminder for past victories and the hope for future winnings even when things were not going too well.

Black theology for the most part, on the other hand, chooses to function as though nothing existed before blacks experienced the dehumanization of slavery; nothing positive or significant went before; nothing praiseworthy and uplifting precedes; no victories worthy of thanksgiving; and as a consequence they must start with the pathology, the slave dirges and the negatives of racism. This could be a mistake both strategically and hermaneutically.

They could start with St. Augustine and the other North African fathers of the church. The first true theologians were Africans. The first true theology was "black" theology. They can start the story with Moses, the native Egyptian, adopted grandson of one of the great pharaohs. These remain vital issues about starting points which should be addressed because the black American is, through his theology, busily cutting himself off from his authentic participation in the larger black story.

Should the proper reconnections be made, pleasant and lofty associations could once more be established between the African of the past, who formed Western civilization by giving the world not only the first theology—the first theology was black and Augustinian,—but mathematics, medicine, etc.

The net result could be the rapid re-description of the nature and value of blacks in God's total plan for the world. Some way must be discovered to state and incorporate into the corpus, the informative body of conventions, the fact that God has already creatively acted through blacks. They have already played some major role in the evolution of theology, philosophy and Western Civilization.

In this sense, blacks with significant status, in control and making noteworthy contributions, represent no new phenomena. We who live today are but part of a continuum, and after a long hiatus, we have been recalled to our rightful place as framers of conscience and builders together with others of God's guidance systems for the total redemption of this sinful world made up of all races.

We need also to remember that even in the areas

related to the very genesis of humanity blacks are at least foreparents to all humans upon the earth today. The inferiority battle was won when it was discovered that the basic genes—DNA—of every man, woman and child in the world today, whatever the race or culture, is directly traceable back to an African mother.

The cover story of "Newsweek" for January 11, 1988, "The Search for Adam and Eve," in living color detailed that the mother of the human race we have today was an African woman. The extended story explains just how modern day science came to such a conclusion.

We share a common mother on earth and a common Father in heaven (never mind the feminists who foolishly wish to make God at once father and mother or hermaphrodite). That our basics came from an African mother, and our "moral add-ons" from a heavenly Father, is a much more logical way of dealing with these issues and certainly congruent with our calling earth Mother Earth from which all life springs and is sustained.

If, indeed, an African woman's DNA is the source of all human life on earth today; if all humans alive today have that African connection, whence is the strange starting point for liberation theology?

All things are already turned upside down. The Overcome battle, a conceptual battle at the core, has been won on this score alone. We may need to "spank" our prodigal children who are rejecting us, writing their parents out of history, depriving them of their birthright, and as it were, placing them in abandoned homes with no lifesaving or life-supporting systems. With such a starting point for all theology, how would it be done? And black theologians have this ace card (concept) that can "trump" the inferior, under mood from which they do their thinking, writing and live their lives. But, they do not use it.

"What Black Liberation Theology Does" is one of the key issues to be addressed in this chapter. Some critics have seen in black liberation theology the formal development of a type of black racism: "A black theology of liberation (of the earlier version of course) can easily be interpreted as a gospel of hate of blacks against whites." [National Baptist Convention][1]

This criticism, laid against some forms of black theology, cannot but set back the "dreams" of some blacks whose Vision Glorious pictures what Martin Luther King, Jr. described, a perfect society in which his little black children will happily hold the hands of their little white friends, living and going to school and church in the same neighborhood. The dream of the integrationist cannot be realized with this kind of talk, this way of looking at the world, intending in the world, hoping and doing in the world.

Another questionable result of black theology, questionable because of the "Vision Glorious"—the success criteria it presupposes is its likeness to Zionism, a type of closed religious ideology that permits no outsider to question its logic, or grammar or inner workings. Blacks are the only jury, and the white reaction must be limited to silent acceptance. James Cone, the father of modern day black theology, said, "If whites were really serious about their radicalism in regard to the black revolution and its theological implications, they would keep silent and take instructions from black people."[2]

Such a comment indicates that extremely limited parameters have been set for black liberation theology, a theology that describes itself as designed strategically for one purpose only, to meet one need, black liberation. It is one of the stranger theologies as developed and argued, for it has no concept of black sinfulness or black redemption from sin.

The question could easily be asked, should blacks gain their liberation today, what would black theology of liberation become tomorrow? But, the key question we must address in this work is the nature of success criteria, the description of the Vision Glorious.

For what we read has no clear indication of what liberation will do; what form it will take or what will count as achievement criteria in this great liberation struggle that has been fought for and for which many books have been now written and many good men have died.

Current black liberation theology is so strategic and pointed because it is geared to achieving one thing, the liberation of black people. A people who were freed one and a half centuries back from legal slavery, but who do not even now celebrate that. And black theology is without any description of that which will mark its work done. This theology has other problems as well, some of which we shall treat elsewhere in this book.

Its themes are never transcultural, examples are never sought elsewhere. Correlations are rarely made with generic human conditions, even peculiar ethnic suffering as experienced by others. If such were done, it might surprise us to note that oppression and suffering are not peculiar to blacks, since there are worse case scenarios in the history of man, cases of man's inhumanity to man, which are in no way peculiar to blacks. One can easily get the impression that there is little in black theology that can transcend and thus become a type of message for all humankind.

Rather, we have a peculiar, historic and strategic theology that leads one to believe that its message is only for the moment, for the peculiar existential situation, and that soon becomes more like preaching, an authentic part of the language of faith, just like the spirituals and the blues, the Psalms, prolegomena to theology, but not theology.

Much of what passes for black theology is more like extended sermons with powerfully relevant messages, but not theology with a logic. Such will remain limited in its applications and occasional in its significance.

Often, black theology, as sermon with a message, rather than theology with a logic, remains heavily social in thrust; and all are asked to accept it because of its social message; and few have dared to bring critical criteria to judge the new enterprise which has fitted itself squarely within the current tendency to socialize all knowledge.

The mixing of a variety of concepts and categories is intricately involved in such thinking and does nothing but further confuse. For the hidden question will forever be raised: what criteria will determine when there is enough politics, socio-economics or whatever will be required before the attainment of the "Vision Glorious," which itself is never adequately pictured, visioned or described?

There is without doubt a need to set criteria, even minimum achievable criteria, the achievement of which will never be dependent on another's agreeing to grant permission or essentially determine the outcome. So, there is the current need for deciding just what is hoped for, what must be satisfied, and by whom such must be satisfied.

THE OVERCOME

Neat statements like, "For black Americans freedom is not a negation, a mere absence of restraints, oppression, or discrimination, but also an affirmation of being, an opening into self-fulfillment and joyful development of latent powers"[3] abound. But, the question comes immediately to mind, who will be the affirming body? Who are the umpires and what beginning creed, story, myth, well-established and accepted standards will be used for the umpiring? I would think that part of the prolegomena of black theology would have to do with the establishment of the basic rules (the grammar if you will) of the exercise at hand.

Assuming that there is a common beginning story might be a major mistake. There is currently none that is generally accepted. And the issue of starting points comes to the fore again. Blacks might need to posit their beginning story in order to get things started. Much more will be said in this regard elsewhere in this work.

What is more telling, however, is the fact that what is being preached as liberation theology cannot itself liberate anyone because the liberator, his language, and way of looking at the world remain trapped. It remains part of the logic of liberation that the liberator himself cannot feel trapped and in the same sinking boat as those to be liberated.

Moses left and went to Midian, gained strength, and returned. Jesus spoke with authority from "outside the trapped" situation and not like the scribes and Pharisees. The would-be liberator must dare to believe and act liberated, if he/she is to lead people to freedom.

These are some of the issues that must be addressed. Since the formation of lives, with new and better ways of looking at the world and intending and doing in the world, is the key feature of any meaningful theology of liberation, black liberation theology cannot continue forever to speak in isolation. If it does, it will remain private, full of many admirable convictions and pronouncements relative to black hopes for redemption, etc. But, there ought to be more. Lives are to be formed in a new mood and key; institutions that support the newly formed lives are to be built and strengthened. Perspectives are to be shaped anew; a redemptive world view fashioned, and none of this could be effectively done by offering more and more points of views on the nature of the pathology.

Where is the uniting story? Where is the starting myth about who we are and how we stand in the world to be found? And, where is the Overcoming/Passover/liberative/event that becomes for all time the interpretive before/after tool that offers a way of managing the otherwise larger than life problem? There seems to persist a false belief that no uniting story/myth is needed as the prior starting point for the properly told black redemptive story.

But, we are at a lost to discover just how black liberationists have assumed that apart from the myth that brings together a motley group of people, sharing only one thing in common, black skins (and many skins not even black for many find the need to call themselves brown, light, dark, etc.), how could such a group be weaved into a community of faith, and what would serve as the criteria for being in or out? As a matter of fact, how does one "enter"? Are there any rites of passage, ritual and liturgy, with correlated creeds and rules for determining status?

Can links be made with other ethnic groups who have suffered and overcome; others who have at one time experienced concentrated acts of dehumanization? For it is one thing to claim that the black experience created a peculiar frame of reference for a special language of faith, enviably expressed through spirituals and black preaching (whites now include many a spiritual in their language of faith). But, to go the further step and set the stage for the conclusion that black liberation theology is only the "descant" on the dirge, the cryings of a suffering people, is quite another matter.

Black liberation thinkers must be forced to make the connections with black suffering across time, and seasons, remembering at least that once in their history, they have been the oppressors, placing "burdens on their slaves so heavy to bear that the God of Israel entered the picture and offered the slaves their Passover event."

Another issue that must be considered has to do with starting points for the liberation enterprise. Should the starting point be only rooted in the black American experience of slavery and the pathological experiences and memories it generates? What will happen when in the larger context other emphases are brought to bare relevant to the existential experience of those doing the theology, or consistent with the myths that inform their self-descriptions?

What happens when the emphasis is sadness/joy; pathetic/lofty self-descriptions; minority/majority status; independent/dependent social contexts, et al, all further complicating the nature of the enterprise, all offering new areas for the development of more and more theologies to answer the abiding question: "What meaneth this?"

One must be reminded that if the context is that which validates the existential questions that must be raised in an effort to gain an appropriate answer from the normative story (the Christian story foremost) and sets the stage for any black liberation theology, then various contexts will force various starting points. I am personally convinced that theology can start anywhere.

It can start with man in his multitude of contextual settings, white, black or other. But, it can also start with God and return to man. But, Christian theology must in the end meet Jesus, the Christ. Herein lies another major problem for all ethnic theologies, for they must deal, as Jesus did, with the generic man in his sinfulness and estrangement from God, while seeking specific examples by looking at the plight of the particular man in the peculiar context.

A theology that refuses to deal with the generic man, but limits itself totally to a specific man in a specific culture, reduces theology to nothing more than another type of cultural expression. If black liberation theology continues to rely on this existential starting point as its only starting point, it could never become transcultural with redeeming point and message for any other.

It could never become the light to enlighten the other Gentiles, and so can become more and more a black ideology doing a good work in raising consciousness among blacks, but with no other redemptive message. And that could be fine. But, much more can and must be asked of the bright minds that are at work here.

Black American theology claims to be liberation theology at its most fundamental level. This is not only a popular claim, but one that has been accepted without any serious analysis of the grammar, the logic, if you will, of liberation theologies and philosophies in general and black liberation thinking in particular.

The key problem with this procedure is that no one is now clear as to the nature and character of the liberation sought. Is the perceived and desired liberation an activity of the mind or of the will? Is it to to be achieved with arms through a series of confrontational activities, or is it a state, something like an achieved condition that sets the stage for a different way of looking at, intending and doing in the world?

A new understanding of the black self that somehow makes him know that he alone ultimately is responsible for his present and his future in terms of valuing, in terms of developing life-saving institutions and communities, in terms of developing a form of life in community much like that envisioned in the Kingdom of God.

What is the nature of the liberation sought, and are its tools Marxist, requiring war with the perceived enemy with whatever weapons are necessary to bring about the new liberated order? And, key to any valuable analysis would be a pointing to what can count as success criteria, the measure for determining the event/moment/conditions that permit the declaration of the victory.

These are some of the problematic questions and issues which I shall address, for they remain problematic and unfinished in the area of black liberation theology and what it does. In this work, I shall make some rather serious attempts at offering pointers to a direction that might offer some hope, and if seriously followed can set the stage for the first and second level of liberation for the black oppressed peoples of the world.

I will show by using conceptual analysis that liberation is not an activity word, pointing to episodes of "struggling" activities to gain liberation, by reminding all that the paradigm of an activity remains, goings-on that have beginnings, middles and endings; doings that could be stopped and started again. In short, doings that could be clocked.

I will demonstrate that to be free and liberated is not in essence activity related, but points more to a status, achieved, that dispositionally poises one to think and do in a different way, the "Overcome/Passover" way. In other words, I plan to show that liberation, black or other, ought to be viewed as an achieved state of being that positions one to do all the things required of liberated, authentically free human beings.

One need not struggle or fight for liberation in the first instance. Using Biblical, political and personal paradigms that show liberation in its pure form, attempts will be made to point a direction in which I think black liberation thinking must go quickly if it is to prove efficacious. I must go this route because, to date, neither the theologians' attempts at making God black and on the side of the poor and oppressed or attempts at making the Christian Redeemer, Jesus, black, have proven efficacious in the black liberation talk.

Using the Biblical story of the Hebrews, one-time slaves in Egypt, dehumanized much like blacks, treated as things, commodities to be used for the well-being of others, their oppressors; remembering that they truly experienced genocide in the deliberate killing of the firstborn males (much as black males are today placed in jails, asked to be the first soldiers in our various Viet Nams; zombied on dope and effectively destroying themselves by homicide and suicide), but the Jews decided to do something about it. They sought their freedom. The Biblical example of liberation from dehumanization is here set in the Bible story of the Exodus. I will show how, after asking permission for freedom, after the many demonstrations (show of resolve, plagues, etc.), the Jews declared and proclaimed their freedom. They went on to develop a story and the appropriate ceremony of Passover, a typology for the Christian resurrection story, their passing over and overcoming the oppression by accepting the total and absolute responsibility for their liberated future.

Reflection on the story will show that there was still no tangible evidence of their liberation, no war at the first level, only a declaration of resolve, a unity of will, and a concerted determination to take their future into their own hands whatever the cost. From that moment, they were truly free and liberated at the first and most fundamental level.

Thereafter, they ran, fought, sought and wrought miracles of survival with the help of their new-found God, who established a covenant between Himself and the people, while requiring them to covenant at the fundamental level of social contract with the basic ten (known to us as the

A BLACK PASSOVER

Ten Commandments). Armed with these brand-new formulations, the Jews went on to overcome one obstacle after another—wilderness, snakes, murmurings, hunger, thirst, war and pestilence—as they worked on several levels to make into a reality what had first only being proclaimed and declared, a type of self-fulfilling prophecy.

Our analysis of the prime political paradigm will in like manner show that the first thirteen American colonies, after various attempts at persuading the ruling power to set them free, even limited freedom from burdensome taxes, simply declared and proclaimed their independence. This was an act of the collective will of those assembled, a statement of common intent, to become henceforth and for all time totally responsible for what their future will be. There were many obstacles yet to be overcome, battles to be fought, amendments to be made to the initial Constitution, laws to be adopted and later adapted, but through the Declaration of Independence, the will to be truly liberated proved to be that first level/stage that would inform and govern their intentions and actions for the future.

Black liberation thinkers have not yet declared this liberative Overcoming/Passover event in a way that could be heard. True that there is a black Declaration of Independence, one that we shall examine and perhaps update in this work, but even with that, blacks as a whole have never proclaimed their liberation as of any time, through any event real or mythical, on their own part or with God's help.

Blacks are, after all the literature and demonstrations, even after the death and elevation of Dr. King, still at the pre-liberation stage of asking permission of the oppressor, the modern-day Pharaoh: "Let my people go."

I want to demonstrate through these pages, through a rich variety of simple, commonsense arguments, using everyday examples, that the liberation of any people must begin with a proclamation and declaration of resolve to take charge, to become responsible for all aspects of their collective future, at whatever costs. A key word is responsibility. For liberation requires this as its chief ingredient.

Black liberation theology would have done its first work when it can identify for its audience its unifying myth or acceptable moment/event in time and history when it declared its liberation—its Overcome/Passover, its Fourth of July, Independence Day, if you will.

I happen to believe such moments are already within the conventions of the black experience.

Black theologians' inability to locate the redemptive event in a black God and His black son, Jesus, may indeed necessitate our movement to creatively develop a theology that works to establish the once-for-all time efficacious understanding of the life, death, and elevation of Martin Luther King, Jr. This then could be used as the unquestionable historical event that could serve, for dating purposes, the moment when the necessary break was made between how we intended, hoped and behaved in the world before and after the declaration of our Overcome/passover event. After our leader's blood has been shed and his after life, larger than life significance, has been elevated and vindicated, things are indeed different.

I shall, therefore, make several arguments to demonstrate the need to interpret the national holiday granted in honor of Martin Luther King, Jr. as the catalyst through which we could easily identify the historical event through which and around which could be developed the unifying liberation myth, the declaration of black independence and the locale of the Overcome/Passover/ moment/event.

From this daring first level of liberation, which also establishes the interpretive break of before/after of our total human experience, we can then as a people begin to look at the vast God-given resources already bequeathed to us, and set out to turn them, through responsible collective action, into the tools that will enable us to demonstrate that what we have declared can be made real.

I shall attempt to offer another approach, from the linguistic philosophers' point of reference, for handling some of the issues fundamental to black liberation theology. The work of most black liberation thinkers is grounded in history, a history of oppression and dehumanization. In short, a history that as it is interpreted by them remains full of negatives, many struggles (activities) to overcome these negatives, but few victories that can be truly celebrated.

As a matter of fact, in my 17 years living in America, I have not yet discovered a festival, a day, a rite, when and through which all black Americans, as a special and as a

A BLACK PASSOVER

peculiar people, celebrate any aspect of life. In celebrating Dr. King's birthday, they have not even developed a rite—fund-raising breakfasts with speeches about past wrongs, come closest to the developing rite. How sad! How ineffectual! How telling of us!

The Jews celebrate some festivals peculiarly significant to them, one being the Passover, through which they overcame slavery and its negatives—through the power of their God working through their Moses and his avenging angel. They walked to the Promised Land, a land envisioned as flowing with milk and honey. They knew when they had arrived, and they could be sometimes triumphant.

Their psalms remind us that they were indeed often triumphant and thankful for achievements and victories over the liberation walk that began with the fashioning, establishing forever of their Passover/overcoming event. But, they were often also sad, scared and disappointed, wondering if God had forsaken them; asking how they could sing the Lord's song in a strange land.

The Irish have St. Patrick's Day, the West Indians do Carnival—in Antigua. On Emancipation Proclamation Day, they celebrate their freedom. And black Americans continue to celebrate nothing, no victories or successes peculiar to their lived lives together.

Perhaps because, to date, there is really no lived lives together. We are indeed waiting for the Overcome. And Dr. King's birthday becomes a day not of celebrating with rite and story anything already achieved through those trailblazers that went before us, but a day for more prayer breakfasts and the day when we sing the leading pre-liberation song, "We Shall Overcome Someday."

I dare, once more, make this prophecy of doom, that apart from our willingness to add moments of celebration, moments of collective thanksgiving for victories already won, for masteries already gained over certain aspects of life; unless we do as a people, at some peculiar time, agreeable to all, acceptable by most, our specific Overcoming event, we cannot make the break (before/after) required for the next stage in our interpretation. Our thinking will then, and forever remain blue, our songs will remain dirges, and our theology will continue to be the descant on the dirge.

Chapter Two Notes

[1] National Black Convention, Cited in Wilmore/Cone, Black Theology, p. 261.

[2] James Cone, *Black Theology of Liberation*, (J. B. Lippincott Co., 1970), p. 119.

Chapter Three

Claim the Ghetto and Build Life-Saving Institutions

As a people, we blacks are given to the description of the evil in our midst, but to date we have not seriously considered it our collective responsibility to do more than point to the pathos and its results. Blacks are indeed very eloquent at describing pathos, but very slow at devising and designing the required range of techniques to manage and heal the perceived pathological situation.

It does appear that a wise and competent people, on recognizing pathological developments within its communities of the magnitude described, would not only talk about the situation (describing), but would actively engage themselves in well-designed strategies that would install the positive change that is sought.

From time to time, we hear pleadings like this:

> If one is to know the agony and the ecstasy of the struggle for social justice for black Americans, he must understand that there are some forces in America which are used to perpetuate poverty, racism, and oppression. White racism is the most explosive problem facing the nation today. Racism has deep roots in our society. It has shaped and determined many of the forms and structures of the basic institutions in America—local and national government, judicial systems, schools, church and family life.

THE OVERCOME

> White racism is a cancer eating away at the very heart of this nation. Racism is rooted systemically in the political practices, value norms and standards of American society, and its role in the shaping of America's economic, political, and cultural institutions has been of central importance. Racism in America is no marginal or isolated phenomenon. It is intrinsic to the American way of life.[1]

If this woeful claim is true, and it must be, since so much of black liberative thinking is actually clearly aimed at white racism, then blacks would better recognize at the outset that their liberation status cannot be built on any foundation or area over which they have absolutely no control. White racism is not the black man's to change. It is not the black man's moral problem. And, it must not be allowed to become the central issue, either.

Rather, white racism should be bled for the positive results that can come from it. It should be used to force on us the need for our peoplehood; the need for our using our exposed $204 billion and the unexposed billions of dollars in our control, as the power lever to leverage significant aid to our institutional development, and in the process, using our blackness, for once, as a recognizing and identifying plus for brotherhood and business and not as the ongoing negative it has come to be.

What is needed at this juncture in black thinking are not more descriptions of the pathology, but pointers to ways out of the entrapment in which blacks find themselves. Consequently, part of what I shall attempt to do is offer such pointers to a way out.

I am convinced that the problems in black society will never be solved until blacks assume the responsibility for their individual and corporate futures with the consequent result of recognizing that the old "bootstrap theory" has a key message for them in their plight.

This should be re-examined to discover whether it contains the potential for helping blacks in the Americas and throughout the world regain some of their lost self-respect, as they demonstrate to themselves first, and the larger world second, that they can indeed recover from the hiatus brought on by their being dislocated from their original culture, from their language and attending ways of viewing and managing their world through the development of the slave trade in recent centuries.

For this to be done, a many-sided approach must be developed if we are to successfully turn around the self-destruct pathological, suicidal trends so well-described and documented by all who have studied the direction of blacks within black communities across America. Initially, the thinking about ourselves; that is, our self-descriptions, our competencies and propensities, must be radically changed and reinformed from a different perspective.

To do this, we must first look at our guidance systems that instruct and form the concepts that in turn govern our lives. I am myself convinced that the major moral (that is, value-giving) guidance system within black communities is the black church.

It is largely through that institution that our common world views are developed, our common ways of seeing, intending, hoping and doing in the world. But, I would dare say that the would-be redemptive institution of the black church, of which I am a part and a leader at that, may itself be one of the root causes of the problem, the key stumbling block to the achievement of liberation of black people in America.

I have said much through that statement, and so must take time to explain (a kind of apology) to my fellow Christian ministers, just what I am getting at when I declare that the church may be the guidance system whose chief guidance modes are truly dysfunctional to the black liberative process.

In other words, the church itself may be the one institution that de facto through its hymns, preaching (interpreting scripture for the day) and its very ethos sets the stage for maintaining blacks in the pre-liberation stage. A stage wherein liberation remains a hope for tomorrow, someday, but not in any sense, even in the theological sense of a foretaste, real and cause for celebration at any time.

I therefore turn to the hymns and preachings, the key language in the black church, for pointers as to how negative descriptions about blacks are developed, reinforced and incorporated into the corpus of conceptual conventions that inform and govern the lives of the people, limiting and framing their perceptions about reality, their hopes and their possibilities.

In the Protestant wing of the black church, where most black Christians are to be found, individual salvation, a saving of the individual and not of the group as a whole, is at the heart of the preaching. Attacks on infant baptisms, the rite of passage for many other Christians, Catholics and orthodox, a rite of welcoming the newborn into the church and community and thereby making all around responsible for its nurturing and well-being, is anathema.

None can in a real sense speak for the other, and the initial erosion of community responsibility for the nurturing and imparting of the values of the society is not reinforced by any rite.

In Jewry, the baby is likewise accepted by a rite of passage, a welcoming into the larger community, with the community collectively assuming the responsibility for the young one, knowing full well that the culture into which the child is now coming like a barbarian invader must somehow be imparted in some consistent way.

A way with some sure and certain rites that would later be extended to lessons attuning the newest "invader" to the values, world view (ways of looking, intending and doing) of the culture. This is done effectively by the telling of the key "stories" and tales, the recounting of the myths that house the values dear to the culture.

Black Protestant churches, with the emphasis on individualism, cannot effectively welcome with ritual and rites the young black invaders of the culture. So they invade, grow up without any introductions into the corporate collective memory of the society.

By age 20, with no other rites of passage to crown years of common instruction about the conventional matrix of values, ways of looking and doing, we find them in jails for violating laws they were never taught to respect. We find them in jail for murdering "brothers" they have called by every other name than brother and for refusing to support children as fathers because they have no concept of fatherhood.

In the area of preaching, the clarion call in many a black church can be caught through this phrase: "You must be saved." To show the dire need for salvation, the preacher often begins his/her litany about the sin and pathology in the society.

The preacher as prophet must indeed do much of this, but the entire process becomes one of "downing" because, unlike other branches with other emphases in Christianity, the black preacher rarely, if ever, reminds his people of their lofty beginnings from which they have fallen.

Rather, the impression is indelibly left on the minds of the people that they are truly wretched, and the pathological examples from the community can prove it. The praise comes only at death, and even then, many ministers cannot bring themselves to call their best members "saints." Rarely, therefore, does the black preacher accentuate anything positive; rarely does he suggest that there is any good to be lifted up, any foundation on which to build community.

Consequently, many leave the church knowing that they are truly evil and good for nothing. Then, the salvation offered by some others is other worldly at the core, for all but the preacher who through his dress, car, jewelry, residence and vacations shows non-linguistically that the things of this world do have their place. And so, we still do have a type of "pie in the sky when you die" message that even today is being preached to some blacks on Sunday.

And the people hear and seem to accept this untimely message, not recognizing that God is the God of the Jews and the whites also. They are very busy claiming dominion over the world, as commanded by God in the Genesis story, where, after He had surveyed His creation, He called it good (yes, even man good at the core).

So we see that the very call for salvation of the otherworldly sort that has become so pervasive sets the stage for the reinforcement of the idea that we are at the core "good-for-nothings," who ought to busy ourselves with the task of taking off to heaven and not making paradise here on earth.

I would strongly suggest that this "being born again" theme shifts its emphasis to asking our people to think again about our plight and our pathology. Then, they should be reminded through that very process that we are now to become responsible for our present and our futures and must begin now to devise whatever techniques, procedures or technologies we deem necessary to save ourselves, our children, our men, our teenage girls from the cycle of hopelessness that governs so many lives in the negative way.

The popular hymns we sing in many of our churches also inform our people in a dysfunctional manner, in so far as they train and tame our minds to think of life chiefly in other worldly terms, in futuristic terms, and worse of all in surrendering terms. Many hymns suggest that all victories, all rewards are in the future: "We Shall Overcome Someday" is one such hymn, dearly beloved by all, held so dear that to say anything about it is very much like touching motherhood.

But, the guidance suggested by the simple interpretation of this hymn is not helpful to a people struggling to overcome the harsh realities that touch their lives.

Elsewhere in this work I show that this very hymn, "We Shall Overcome Someday," must be changed to signal the Overcoming/Passover event pre-required for blacks as they shift from the pre-liberation state of hoping of overcoming to the liberation status of knowing and behaving in the temper and mood of a liberated people.

A cursory look at the Bible's Exodus story, which recounts the overcoming by the Jews of slavery and the degradation that accompanies slavery, would demonstrate that the Passover event was indeed a declaration of having overcome when there was no real evidence of having overcome.

When the Jews declared their Passover, they were still in Egypt, they were still slaves. But, rather than sing psalms and hymns about the hope for overcoming some day in the future, they proclaimed and declared their independence and freedom, developed an appropriate ritual called the Passover, and accepted the responsibility for their collective future. The Jews did not stop there, however. They went on to work with zeal to demonstrate that what had been proclaimed could be made into a formidable reality.

In this very initial consideration of this issue lies many of the conceptual problems that confront blacks, conceptual problems that trap them and hold them back. Built into this is the misunderstanding of just how prophetic language can be made to mean differently at different times in history as the contextual setting changes. Consequently, blacks are comfortable with the initial interpretations of hymns like "We Shall Overcome Someday" done effectively by black preachers of yesteryear when such was indeed the right strategy for saving an entire people from what would have been certain genocide.

And, it would have been a certain genocide had they not adopted the quietening style during otherwise revolutionary gatherings; had they not demonstrated through their songs that they had no intentions of at that stage taking anything away from their oppressors because their minds were set elsewhere, their true rewards were elsewhere.

They would not even get drunk and change their minds, for liquor was evil. Neither would the strong black man "seduce" the other woman, for the church was definitely against wine, woman and song. We pray God's richest blessings on the wise, old time black preacher who developed this life-saving strategy, saving our race from certain genocide and preserving us for a day like this.

But the prayer must continue that God will enlighten the contemporary preachers to the point where they recognize that different times require updated emphases.

Gayraud S. Wilmore's assessment of black churches' current stance in comparison to the black church of the last century is as telling as it is condemning:

> The black church of the nineteenth century, despite its 'client' relationship to white churches, was clearer about its identity than many of us today. It knew itself to be God's judgment upon the inhumanity of racism. Its blackness was, therefore, an expression of its sense of cultural vocation. By every measure it was an amazing institution. Led for the most part by illiterate preachers, many of whom were slaves or recent freedmen, poverty stricken and repressed by custom and law, this church converted thousands, stabilized family life, established insurance and burial societies, founded schools and colleges, commissioned missionar-

ies to the far corners of the world, and at the same time agitated for the abolition of slavery, supported illegal actions in behalf of fugitives, organized the Underground Railroad, fomented slave uprisings, promoted the Civil War, developed community political education and action in behalf of civil rights, and provided the social, economic, political, and cultural base of the entire black community in the United States.[2]

Compared with their work, under their most difficult circumstances, the contemporary black church, with its educated leadership, living in an age when the law is on its side, when its members are no longer seen as three-fifths of a man, is doing a superbly embarrassing job.

We are surely not building in the tradition of our great forebears, and in many cases we are busily dismantling, or standing by with whimpish cries while others dismantle, institution after institution, built by our foreparents—hospitals, insurance companies, colleges, etc.

Our watch has been one that supervised the demise of institutions built by foreparents and handed down to us. And if Wilmore is correct, part of the Overcome challenge will have to do with calling us to continue to build (and not destroy) life-saving and sustaining institutions, an enterprise begun by our rather uneducated and unsophisticated foreparents, just out from slavery, and destroyed by our modern day, educated, upwardly mobile blacks, preachers and preached to, together.

There is clearly a recognition that the black contemporary church is falling short in many key areas. And, much of the criticism is coming from within the church itself:

> When one views the contemporary black church, it becomes abundantly clear that its main purposes, with one exception, do not serve the needs of the people who attend these churches; but quite the contrary, they serve the needs of the larger exploitive society. Since this is the case, the black church can be easily indicted for having failed to meet its institutional responsibility to the black community. The

> function of an institution is to organize in as effective a pattern as possible, those customs, practices of a community that aid in its survival and stimulate it in its growth. Therefore, the function of the religious force is to organize those customs, practices and understandings that the community has embodied as its most important reality. This reality must define and clarify this particular community's reason for remaining a group. It must strengthen the individual's reasons for living as a positive and creative part of the society. The religious institution should make it possible for the wisdom of one generation to be passed on to the next. It should embody truths and experiences that clarify the pitfalls that cause the breakdowns in human relationships...and the religious institution, together with other black institutions, failed in its responsibility to develop a viable culture.[3]

We are, of course, in agreement with this description of our past failures, but we want to have no ongoing part to play in eternally recounting and re-describing what is wrong and how we failed us.

This is another reason for dedicating this book toward the effort of establishing the black Overcoming/Passover event through which we recognize these and all other failures, wherever chronicled, as part of our pre-liberation, pre-overcoming way of talking about and doing things.

Now we are being prepared, as an Overcome people, to recognize the need for building every life-saving and sustaining institution; for lifting up those who went before and showed us the way, preparing the model for us; a time when we support, with patience and resolve, the task of beginning once again to build those life-saving institutions—establishments our recent forebears, just out of slavery, understood and did with greater success and effect than the modern black man.

My suggestion is that immediately after the doing of Overcome/Passover, with appropriate rite, blacks move to become less tribal. This can be accomplished if blacks merge themselves into a cohesive group, with the black church and other tribal groupings showing the way, as they wake up to the task of helping to accomplish the needed unity of black peoples, the world over. The fresh start heralded by and through the declaration of the black Overcome must then be seen as all that is needed.

We will never need to begin again, for the-once-and-for-all-time significance of the Overcome, which establishes the break between the under/over years of black development, means that never again will we, our children or their children's children, find themselves in the pre-liberation, irresponsible state of always and forever asking for permissions even to describe themselves, to create value or take total charge of their futures.

This book is being written, under inspiration, I hope, to lead us to the realization that the hymn, "We Shall Overcome Someday," must at some point in the evolution of black thinking and black religion be changed to become, "We Have Overcome Today."

That must be the first stanza, representative of our religious Declaration of Independence through the identification of our Overcome/Passover event, and that first affirmative stanza may be followed by others, reminding us that much work is yet left to be done. Part of the logic of this suggestion is the same as that which is contained in the theory about "self-fulfilling prophecy."

In this procedure, the desirable description or outcome is presented as the already established norm and normative. Persons are consequently challenged to match it, to make it true. And it works.

The Jews did just that while in slavery, and thereafter ran through the Red Sea, worked their way through wildernesses and deserts, fought countless battles through which they developed the core for building success myths around named heroes; they survived racism and the Holocaust, while miraculously keeping intact all the ingredients required to rebuild family and community.

The first 13 colonies in these United States started something grand and revolutionary with a simple Declaration of Independence. The moment before the declaration and the moment after had very little if anything in terms of physical, measurable evidence that would set them apart.

A BLACK PASSOVER

There was nothing that established the clear line of demarcation of "before/after" of pre-liberation/liberation, except that document proclaiming their resolve to determine what their future would be. In that very act they made themselves responsible for all vital aspects of their future. Such is the nature of true liberation and independence.

As a people in America, blacks have never done this. Their talk, even their liberation talk, has not yet come close to this simple, but absolutely revolutionary stance. Their hymns quietly inform them that in some future time, through the work of some future liberator, the victory over oppression will be won.

And so, the pre-liberation state is continued into the indefinite future. I must argue from a variety of standpoints the absolute necessity for blacks to do the required first thing of declaring their having overcome through the struggles and victories of our liberators, then go on from that point to demonstrate to ourselves first, and the world second, the reality already proclaimed to mark the beginning of the first positive self-fulfilling prophecy within the total black community.

Then, there is that dear old hymn we all love to sing, "His Eye's on the Sparrow," very touching on one level, very dysfunctional on another for a people who remain "under." Why? It picks the lowest picture of who we are in the eyes of God, sparrows with puny legs and wings. True that this picture is quite Biblical.

But, there are much more lofty pictures of who we are: sons and daughters of God, joint heirs and inheritors of the kingdom of God; creatures made but a little lower than the angels to be crowned with glory and honor; man, made good in creation and commanded in the formative myths about our beginnings to "have dominion over the world"; brothers and sisters worthy for Christ to come and make his abode with us (Incarnation), die for us (Passion/Easter) event.

Such pictures are also to be found within the body of Christian conventional ways of describing themselves before God. Despite these uplifting pictures, however, there seems to be some built-in propensity to choose images that show blacks as lost, worthless or very low. Until a concerted move is made to shift the imagery used to describe blacks by blacks, the stage will not be set for declaring our "having overcome," the prerequisite for assuming the total responsibility for our common futures.

For if we continue to describe ourselves in lowly rather than lofty terms, who will believe that there is any power within ourselves to help ourselves? I happen to believe that people are not so much what they eat as what they think, and if such lowly self-effacing self-descriptions are forever fed the minds of a people, slowly and by osmosis, they will indeed become what they have been led to think.

The church, while it remains the major guidance system within our black communities, cannot, however, be asked to do all the work in the effort to set the mood and ready the minds of a people for accepting the total responsibility for developing whatever technologies are necessary to save its communities and the peoples within them.

The people must be called upon to pay attention to the names they call each other. A walk through any of these communities will reveal that awfully demeaning names are used to describe fellow blacks by blacks. The very names they hate others to call them are used as common parlance, and even today, if you are an honest reader, we will all admit that "you black so and so," used as often as it is, speaks to the fact that to be black in the minds of those who curse with the word "black" must be in some sense sinister.

We must return to the warning that blacks must indeed watch the names they call each other, for naming sets the stage for all types of relationships.

Call the police "pigs" as the Black Panthers did, and one can easily hurt or kill the police; call the Asians "gooks," and we can kill them with ease; as in the same vein calling blacks "niggers" once set the stage for maltreatment and other forms of dehumanization.

We must begin to improve on the types of names we use in our communities if we are to begin to see ourselves as brothers and sisters ready to declare our Overcoming in reality what we have eloquently declared to be pathological in our common lives together.

As mentioned before, one of the first steps in the redemptive exercise for blacks is the re-description of our-

A BLACK PASSOVER

selves in the proper light, permitting ourselves by the very descriptions we offer of ourselves to believe that like other peoples, like the Jews in particular, we can assume the responsibility for our futures.

This process might require that we re-do that portion of our history that tends to stop us and confirm historically that we are recently out of slavery, that short period in our history when we were the enslaved and not the enslaver as we had been of one another and of other races. We once enslaved the Jews in Africa. Egypt is in Africa, you would remember. We were hard taskmasters.

Like the Greeks, we need to go back if only through mythological heroes to the golden years of black rule and power in Egypt and North Africa when black pharaohs developed civilizations whites will never bring themselves to attribute to our genius and having done this while Europe was yet truly barbarous.

We need to contemplate the fact that Africa fathered and mothered[4] Western Civilization by giving it its first philosophy and Christian theology, geometry, and the concept of the zero that made possible the development of modern calculations. Watch Great Britain shift from pounds/shillings/and pence to pence that are actually percents.

Such may serve to remind us that there is somewhere a past dignity that we owe it to our forebears to recover and pass on to our children. The hope being that each young black man and each young woman will begin to see himself and herself as a mighty pharaoh, a bright St. Augustine of Hippo, setting the theological stage for all God-talk in the Western world, and knowing that the time has come for us as a race of people to recognize that we must pick up where these great men left off as we reclaim our positive place in history and not remain a dispensable footnote.

What is then required after we have re-described ourselves as a valuable and competent people who laid the foundations of Western Civilization through our great thinkers? What after we upgrade the names by which we call each other? What after we flag the message in some of the hymns we now sing and reinterpret and update them?

What after we force our preachers to bring us messages becoming of sons and daughters of God, made in God's image and but a little lower than the angels? What after we have declared our having overcome, and through that action accept the total responsibility for our individual and corporate futures?

In what follows an attempt will be made to offer some more pointers as to specific directions for the future and projects that can be developed to demonstrate the working out of the declaration of our having overcome. Through the process of doing this, some general picture of the "Vision Glorious," which would count as success criteria in the recent struggle for liberation, should begin to emerge.

Re-description of Resources

We are not a poor people. This statement may indeed shock many who have been trained to believe that blacks in America are best described as "poor, black and in real trouble." Nothing could be further from the truth. For despite any negative picture others may offer, and we accept, the fact remains that blacks, in America, as a group, are not poor.

There are about 30 million blacks in America, roughly 12 percent of the population. This group has a purchasing power, well-documented, in excess of $204 billion. This represents massive and awesome economic power that exists, but is not being harnessed for the collective benefit of blacks.

With blacks, there has been a traditional tendency to do little to advance themselves socially and economically, and this failure has played its part in impeding any significant impact on the quality of our own lives. Because we have tended to remain mostly consumers and not producers and are given to pursuing independent activities as individuals, our efforts remain truly impotent, further lessening any meaningful effects, as we remain passive while others use our dormant assets to advance themselves.

The estimated $204 billion in purchasing power held by blacks in America, when placed in economic perspectives, exceeds the combined dollar value of all business done between the United States and Japan/China/Russia. Spending by black America was estimated at the $160 billion level in 1983. Seen in this light, blacks are not poor, but themselves have the resources needed to change their plight. They remain a people without economic power, mainly because their national integrating organizations have been given to advocacy of one sort of another, but never effectively to economic empowerment.

Their major guidance systems have never developed in the people the right attitudes to money, consequently they have never been able to develop the networking of economic resources within their communities that would facilitate the flow of the money within that particular community.

Consequently, we discover that whereas in Jewish communities the economic networking of which we speak permits money to turnover seven times before exiting; in the larger white community, money is turned over about five times before leaving, but in black communities, we find a situation wherein money turns over 1.5 times before leaving.

When money, the "secular sacrament of life," leaves a community at such a rapid rate, it certainly cannot serve the varied needs of the community with the same result as is occurring in the other communities. This one fundamental fact, I think, is the key reason for the perceived and actual plight in black communities.

For money, which is the sacrament of life in a country like ours, is not channelled in ways that will permit it to do its salvation work within our black communities. The preacher's money, earned in the black community, rarely goes to a black anything: bank, butcher, supermarket, shoemaker, insurance firm, landlord or mortgage holder.

His money, often made from mites and tithes collected from the black poor, has no systematic channels through which it could be circulated within the community in return for good services.

The consequence is always the same. The billions owned by blacks quickly return to the networking control of those who have methodically put systems in place to channel the flow of cash in a given society in return for services, with the net result of each feeding and serving the other, another way of securing community interdependence and cohesion.

The task may seem great, perhaps even overwhelming. One may even inquire whether anything can be done to change the depressing situation. My question would be: "Is the planning of our future too great a task for us? Can we put something this vital into the hands of others?" I dare say, no. But, despite the massiveness of the task ahead, we can begin now by looking at the entire picture, by truly assessing all aspects of the situation, and then we can choose one small, manageable aspect and conquer that (overcome it) and so celebrate and move on to others.

None of this can begin to happen in any significantly redemptive way before we accept the responsibility for its success or possible failure as a corporate body. After this recognition, it becomes evident from the outlined facts that we have collectively all the resources we will need; what we truly need is the concerted will. Hence, once more, the new description of ourselves as competent and able—as trusting and wise—as resourceful and ready—becomes important.

A new church ethos, one that emits a consciousness of a common mission, fed by a uniting story, even a mythological story, will be needed to guide the people out of the mess of mistrust and hopelessness into the state of busy industry as we devise the technology that is required to manage the work at hand.

I have so far been suggesting that we need very much to place our economic well-being and combined economic power at the top of the scale of our priorities. But, that many-sided approach of which I spoke earlier must be always held in mind. Our practice has been one that would take one issue at a time.

Consequently, we once identified education as the goal and invested all in that aspect of our being. Well and good. But, we soon discovered that we needed some politics and civil rights to go along with the education. So we did. Now, we might be recognizing that money, involvement in the economy on several levels (not just as consumers), is also required. I dare say that perhaps we should have gone after the money first since money can buy education, political favors and most other commodities that are for sale in the society.

My justification for the bold attack advocated here on the problem blacks face comes in part from my contemplation of the real significance of the gifts they brought to the baby Jesus—gold, frankincense and myrrh. These gifts, for Christians, who respect the story that contains them, must have some relevance for us today. I venture to offer an interpretation which should be helpful in creating the theological framework for our thinking about the various aspects of our everyday lives, which must be held together at all costs.

Gold, we can all readily agree, points to the need for glitter and splendor; the need for money to make possible good things, even the good thing of offering tithes to the church, offering relief to the poor and paying for life-saving medicines to help keep us whole in body.

Then, there is frankincense, connected as it is with the worship of God in the temple, with the education that was offered through temple and synagogue and the wisdom generated from this source for management of money and the rest of life.

But, there was another gift, myrrh. Myrrh is an embalming substance used to prepare the dead for burial. Should one give this as a gift to a baby? A gift of gold, with intentions and wishes for wealth, power, and glitter, is fine. A gift of incense with best wishes for knowledge from God and wisdom to manage the affairs of life is also fine. But, a gift of myrrh is in a sense a death wish.

This final gift is, however, a part of life's picture. Along with the glitter of gold and the knowledge gained from walking with God comes the pathos, pain and death. And, it does appear to me that this message is central and key. Pathos is indeed a part of the picture, but it must never be viewed as the entire picture, complete only with sad songs and dirges, with no glitter and no cause for praise and thanksgiving.

No one aspect of our being is to consume us. Each is given, as it were, in an effort to aid us in creating the type of balance required. The type of management skills required must be developed. I dare say that blacks have an overdose of pathology, a reasonable amount of knowledge, enough gold to get going, but no overriding story to pull it all together and make it meaningful.

One aspect of what is most needed in the redemptive event of blacks is a new way of viewing what is already theirs, what has already been achieved, so that some of the glittering, successful aspects of life, worthy to be celebrated and to become the occasion of thanksgiving, may be identified and lifted up.

We must begin now to do whatever is possible to bring the glittering aspects of life into the balancing out of our lives that are presented currently as being top heavy with pathology and laden with the wrong type of knowledge and practical wisdom.

The development of thought has as its one intent, the reader will notice, the placing of the total and absolute responsibility for the changes required in the black community squarely on our collective shoulders. And so, in what follows, some attempt will be made to offer directions as to the "how" of collective survival.

If we were to use the Jews as both ancient and contemporary examples, we would discover that over their history they have suffered as much as have blacks, if not more. They, too, were slaves, slaves to black pharaohs in Egypt who, according to the Exodus story, made their burden very heavy indeed.

They, too, were condemned to dwell in ghettos. As a matter of fact, the word was first used in relationship to Jewish isolation in the ghettos of Europe. They were identifiable and were discriminated against—no Jews, no dogs, no blacks. They also had a language problem, and contrary to popular belief, many came to this country poor.

Yes, the Jews had to leave everything behind, in some cases trading all their material possessions for their freedom. Attempts were made in this century to wipe them out as a race, and the events of the Holocaust remind us of the concentrated and effective campaign to eliminate the Jewish race from the face of the earth.

But they have survived. They have overcome and have built themselves such communities that presidents listen to appeals from Jews about Israel, though their numbers are comparatively few. But, presidents totally ignore the cries of blacks regarding Haiti and South Africa.

Why? Power, economic power. And how was that gained? Well, unlike blacks, who hate their environs and run from them, the Jews accepted, if even for a duration, their ghetto residence, and they used their time there well. They built one life-saving institution after another

A BLACK PASSOVER

and honed in on the perfection of community-building skills, perfecting their skills in commerce, banking, hospital management, service delivery, strong family ties and excellent community support systems.

They developed networking systems for the internal use of the "initial" little they had in terms of resources and wisely and cooperatively made it to grow to the point where they can now command the attention of politicians and presidents.

I am myself convinced that many Jewish people have succeeded precisely because they built every life-saving institution necessary to their well-being and in and through that process became employers of their own people. Hopelessness could not be the dominating ethos. Their sons and daughters never needed government summer jobs to teach them good work habits and offer pocket change for the cinema.

The community had that built in through the rich variety of profit and non-profit institutions which could employ at all levels—from top management for the brightest and best, to positions of janitor and handyman, for those thus inclined. Jobs and to spare; support and to spare; skills well-honed to be taught and passed on within families; money galore for education and politics, for charity and to buy themselves more pleasing communities, when the time was right.

Blacks, on the other hand, have never been able to describe the ghetto as God's gift of a controlled "lab" in which to develop institutions, techniques, communities, jobs, supportive family life and appropriate rites of passage within the society and to enter the society.

Rather, we have tended to see it as a trap, a prison, with nothing but negative connotations, a place to "run away from" at the very first opportunity.

The ghetto for blacks is a place without value and without opportunity. And, we continue to see the places where most of our homes are located as places without value until re-gentrification, the coming back of the whites to reclaim and update that which was given to us and never valued, scares us into recognizing that the constitution of the ground in the ghetto is no different from that on which the White House stands.

It could even be that the constitution of the ground in

the ghetto has something on the grounds of the White House, scientifically. We soon realized that the controlling attitudes and dispositions of those who are in control have more to do with the prevailing perceptions and valuings than does anything else.

The call, therefore, is one that asks us to re-describe where we live as labs from which and in which we will develop all the technologies necessary to operate successfully on the pathological society we now have. Blacks must claim the ghetto as their first territory, and they must do it now in our various Harlems before Rockefeller revisits and claims valuable real estate so close to the overcrowded downtown centers.

The call is one that asks that we see the ghetto, not only as the God-given lab, but also as island, surrounded perhaps by hostile enemies who wish our failure. But recognizing that because we are wealthier in purchasing power than three-quarters of the nations upon earth, we can slowly and methodically develop the supportive and empowering institutions that will become in time the foundation of our beginning network.

This is a network for the turning over of our capital—the chaining of our monies through the hands of fellow blacks for well-rendered services and well-delivered goods—not five or even seven times as is the case in white Gentile and Jewish communities, but ten times, because there is so much catching up to do.

To put this another way, blacks must claim the ghettos as their first conquered land after declaring their Overcoming/Passover and walking into their future Promised Land. This process requires that we teach black people how to do their own valuing, rather than wait for others to do their valuing for them.

What processes can we use to combat the forces that are so well-ingrained in order to overcome the mindset in light of the fact that the problems are so massive and the further fact that what is being proposed here is neither new in conception nor in terms of isolated attempts to make them work?

I suggest that we quickly learn concepts of mutuality and move to mutual funds and investment clubs; that we quickly learn the concept of cooperation and move to cooperatives and corporations; that we quickly learn that

A BLACK PASSOVER

no man is an island, and the death of each black man at the hand of his brother diminishes us all. The task must be undertaken despite the risk, and all this must be done by blacks for blacks, and now. For if not us, who? And if not now, when? Someday!

I further propose that the church in each community identify one or two aspects of states of affairs that ought to exist within our "Vision Glorious" held for the redeemed black community. Such could be profit or non-profit locally-based institutions that could be designed to hire small or large numbers of people, members of the church or others, and that that church raise money specifically to get that operation going as its first tangible contribution to the networking of life-saving institutions required in our communities.

The millions, if not billions, now raised through churches are not set to work to continue anything but our ministers' living expenses and the subsidiary supports he/she might need—secretary, sexton, music, teachers, etc. This can all change rapidly if we committed ourselves to this other aspect of our life-saving task.

The task that would put back some measure of self-respect, some evidence of achievement, in our people, reversing the "I can't do this feeling" with tangible evidence that "I have already done that. Look and see."

Of course, I return to the main theme of this work and remind the reader that we should collectively decide to use Martin Luther King, Jr. and his life and story as the beginning date for our new approach to life. So, we make it significant as representing the break, the before and after of our development process. And, we target the Jews as our example of how a people can, with a Passover event celebrated by most of them annually, overcome time and again   all obstacles.

Notes for Chapter Three

[1] Address of Joseph A. Johnson, Bishop, Fourth Episcopal District of the Christian Methodist Episcopal Church, 1970. Cited in Wilmore/Cone, *Black Theology*, p. 280.

[2] Gayraud S. Wilmore, Ibid., p. 244.

[3] Position Paper by Philadelphia Council of Black Clergy, 1968, cited Ibid., p. 277.

[4] January 11, 1988 issue of "Newsweek" suggested that an African woman is the mother (Eve) of all mankind because her DNA is to be found in all humans. Cover story.

Chapter Four
Black Liberation: More Than Consciousness-Raising

What has black liberation theology accomplished other than black consciousness-raising?

This question is implied in the following, taken from Manos Buthelezi's work. "Was Christ's resurrection not sufficient to liberate you, black man, from that kind of spiritual and psychological death?"[1]

This is a key question in the critique of black liberation theology. For even after making God and His Jesus black, blacks continue to live and sing, "We Shall Overcome Someday."

We must, in moving beyond this point, take the argument and the pre-liberation movement of these theologians and liberationists one step further and either declare 1) our having overcome in Jesus (black or other once and for all time) or 2) declare our political, cultural, psychological and economic liberation through Martin Luther King, Jr.

In so doing, we will effectively create the one thing I advocate in this book, the establishment of the before and after that can place a cry of frustration, like this disparate statement from the Episcopal Address to the 27th General Conference of the Christian Methodist Episcopal Church: "The history of the black man in America has been one of endless struggle against the forces of racism, oppression and exploitation.

"After four hundred years of enslavement of our fathers, the black man today still remains on the fringe of society, deprived, decitizenized. We are no longer held in physical bondage, but we are none the less bound by a history of social, economic, and cultural oppression which has been more damaging in its effects than physical enslavement.

"The black man in America has used a variety of strategies and programs. We have tried the vocational education programs of Booker T. Washington, the legal persuasion of the NAACP, the emigrationism of Marcus Garvey, the moral and ethical persuasion of Martin Luther King, Jr. However, we are still oppressed. Even though some progress has been made, yet we remain on the fringe of American society. We are politically, socially, economically and culturally enslaved."[2]

The address continues to outline further the depth of the desperation that key leaders in the black community feel: "The situation of the black man in America is desperate and baffling. Our situation is radical, unique and complicated. It requires new strategies, new programs, new philosophies and new interpreters. It requires a new orientation of the black man's thinking about the society in which he lives and about himself."[3]

Again, the need for a new way of seeing, intending, hoping and doing in the world of black experiences is eloquently stated. The recognition is there of the many failed programs, the many tried and failed approaches. The pattern is one of trying, failing and filing the failure as we move to the next trial.

What I offer could also fail. It could be filed and recorded, but never instituted in a manner that can effect change.

Some may inquire about my authority to dare to offer the Overcoming/Passover as the means of gaining the interpretive handle and the means of starting again from a dated beginning and building all as if from scratch—who authorizes this?

Logic. The grammar of the black man's plight; the logical geography of his total pathological situation, as described by him, says that a new dated start, after the process of assuming the responsibility this time for success or failure, demands this.

I dare raise and answer this question because Edward K. Braxton, in his article, "Toward a Black

Catholic Theology,"[4] pointed to and raised the question about authority. "What constitutes an authentic black experience? Who constitutes the accrediting agency for genuine blackness? Who gives the stamp of approval, if you will, to someone's postures, attitudes, points of view, as being genuinely black?"

The issues raised are indeed potent, and so long as approaches offered as the interpretive handle on the black problem are seen as "points of view" or "someone's postures" as Braxton tends to do here, the establishment of the normative matrix for black liberation will forever elude.

Gaylord Wilmore recognized the need for a unifying "something" that would get us started towards peoplehood, where before we were no people. He says:

> The central purpose of the new black theology movement in the United States, as well as in the Caribbean and South Africa, was not to glorify black skin color and promote a new form of black racism, but to impel a crisis of identity which could reawaken in black people a belief in their historical individuality as providential and bind the spiritual power generated by the renewed sense of peoplehood to the vocation of cultural decolonization and political liberation. The history of God's liberating acts, from the Exodus to the mission of Jesus, provided a paradigm of a gathered nation, a people 'who were no people,' often faithless and disobedient, but called through suffering and sacrifice to demonstrate that God delivers the oppressed and 'to him who has no might increases strength.' (Isa 40:29)[5]

Wilmore is on the right track. Something must be made to count as adequate for getting us started on our peoplehood; something must be identified as authentic and efficacious.

We must build up a body of conventions, that enriched cultural base, that can in turn become the source of our success criteria and give birth to our fundamental paradigm. In a real sense, after declaring our

THE OVERCOME

Overcoming in Christ (spiritually if Christian) and Martin Luther King culturally, psychologically, economically and politically, we shall need quickly to go about the business of developing and depositing into our new matrix of conventions—the Overcome form of life—a wide range of brand-new concepts befitting our new-found persona in the Overcome/Passover era.

To date, the frustration and desperation continues because we remain on the wrong side of Passover, paralyzed by a strange inability to sing the Overcome song and through that simple act be transformed as we enter stage one of the liberated era.

To date, as expressed elsewhere, all our sighing, all our thinking, all our praying, all our intending, all our hoping is truly descriptive of a pre-liberated people. And Bishop Johnson's frustrations are truly felt and understood. But, they can never be corrected until we grant ourselves the permission, despite questions about whence the authority, as raised by Braxton, to create, date and institute our Overcoming/Passover event.

We must seize this authority, from the body politic, and institute Overcome/Passover in and through whomever person and event. So, once more, we establish that much-needed before and after, that dynamic interpretive tool, we need now in order to handle the situation in which we find ourselves.

Black liberation theology is, for the most part, grounded in the historical reflection on the last four hundred years' experience of blacks in America, including the slave experience.

The history is morbid and depressing, evoking anger and despair as can be evidenced from the expressions on the faces of young blacks who viewed the television series "Roots." Whereas the Jewish youngster, viewing a movie on the Holocaust comes from it with the idea that such must be remembered in an effort to reinforce the "never-again" theme, the black youngsters, viewing a part of his story in "Roots," demonstrates chiefly anger and despair.

And so we believe that black liberation thinking, rooted as it is in vivid pathological descriptions of its total experience, with no moment of victory, no pause for true celebration, cannot save itself apart from the introduction of another approach to the problem through which what

A BLACK PASSOVER

is seen as an overwhelming problem is transformed conceptually into a problematic issue that can be analyzed, placed in proper perspective and managed or overcome.

Black theology and black consciousness-raising are considered by some to be identical. "The two movements are in fact synonymous, for both are concerned with the liberation of the total black man."[6]

> Black theology means the taking of resolute and decisive steps to free black people not only from estrangement from God, but also from slave mentality, inferiority complex, distrust of themselves and continued dependence on others culminating in self hate.[7]

That black theology is an appeal to the black man to overcome his slave mentality is the recurring theme in much of the writings of black theologians. The most potent weapon in the hands of the oppressor remains the mind of the oppressed. The black man is enslaved by his own thinking and attitudes even more effectively than by his enslavement by any power outside himself. He has learned to think white, to buy white, to bank white and to equate white with valuable.

To a large degree, he has been accepted as human only in so far as he has rejected "black" ideals and accepted "white" ideals. This led to the acceptance by blacks of the "colonized mentality as they became more and more controlled by a masochistic complex," the victim of self-hatred and self-loathing.[8] However, much of this has been radically altered, partially due to the rise of black theology.

Slowly, but surely, the black man is rediscovering his somebodyness. He seems no longer totally willing to live according to white descriptions of humanity, only. And some are clearly asking that we find ways to acknowledge those things which we cannot change, such as the giveness of our skin color, and concentrate on the things that we can drastically change, such as our attitudes to ourselves and the key ways in which we describe ourselves and live.

Black theology and black consciousness-raising are

very closely connected. The chief result of black theology has been black consciousness-raising. From it has issued many well-formulated, quotable statements, further evidence that for the most part, blacks tend to believe and behave as though the "saying" of a thing constitutes its being instituted and effective.

And so, we have many wise sayings that state the issue, like: "Black theology means taking resolute and decisive steps to free black people not only from estrangement from God, but also from slave mentality, inferiority, distrust of themselves and continued dependence on others culminating in self-hate."[9] But, it seems to stop with the saying or stating of the fact.

Black theology of liberation, more accurately called African-American theology of liberation, remains disconnected from past African culture. Slavery did break that cultural link and created a new black man (of the Diaspora) across the Atlantic. If the reconnection of all blacks is to be made for our total corporate salvation, then it is time to bridge with language, the language of fact, history and interpretive myth where facts and extra factual truths merge and are made to mean—the gap.

Myths that give interpretive meaning and purpose, perspective if you will, to black life, inclusive of its golden past (documented wherever possible or extracted from stories about our heroes) our slave experience, a troubled present and a promising future are to be established and inculcated.

What must be overcome through black liberation theology? "Black theology is an appeal to the black man to overcome his slave mentality" because it is recognized by all that the most effective means of maintaining oppression is the dormant, accepting mind of the oppressed.[10]

"The black man is enslaved by his own thinking and attitudes even more effectively than by his enslavement to any power outside himself. He has been taught to think 'white.'" "He has been accepted as human only in so far as he has rejected 'black' ideals and accepted 'white' ideals...the victim of self-hatred and self-loathing."[11]

Black theology as black consciousness brought blacks to the point of discovering and recognizing their somebodyness as Martin Luther King points out and so

A BLACK PASSOVER

some are ready to change the definition of humanity that excluded them for so many years back to one that fully includes them. The new appeal, as cited by David Bosch,[12] demands: Let us claim and affirm those things which we cannot change (such as our blackness) and acknowledge those things we can change (such as our attitudes to blackness). But, attitude change is not enough. Our full-fledged Overcoming/Passover event, complete with its Vision Glorious, must be put in place and now. For we recognize that:

> Black power is a call for black people in this country to unite, to recognize their heritage, and to build a sense of community. It is a call for us to take the initiative, to build the kind of community which crosses all class lines and geographical lines, in order that the resources and leadership of all black people may be used. Black power means the development and utilization of the gifts of black men for the good of black men and the whole nation.[13]

It remains a great pity that these great statements of purpose remain only statements. Consider again the following statement:

> The black revolution is a fact. It is a call for black people throughout the nation and the world to stand on their own feet and declare their independence from white domination. The mood of the day is for black people to throw off the crippling myths of white superiority and black inferiority. The old myths are being replaced by black pride, self-development, self-awareness, self-respect, self-determination and black solidarity.[14]

What beautiful statements blacks make. A quotation like this should have been made true by now. But those who "say" such nice things tend to believe that in the saying of the thing is the doing of the thing. Nothing could be further from the truth. As we indicated elsewhere, the saying, like the praying, simply frames and sets the parameters for appropriate actions and behaviors. But, to date, all these correct "sayings" about what the black situation should be, sayings which remain far apart from the socio-economic, psychological, political realities, remain such for precisely one reason.

We know that such and such should be the case. We might even know, for the most part, how to achieve our "desired ends." But the "page break" with the old way of seeing, talking, doing, hoping, intending, etc. has not yet been established.

We have not yet brought the old ways to an end in time, with a date and through an event. So they have not been stopped, even symbolically. Hence they have not been overcome. And the new way of talking, hoping, doing and judging cannot yet be installed effectively. Hence our cry and appeal to the powers that be, Jesse Jackson and Stevie Wonder and Bill Cosby, to help us do the first thing first. Establish once and for all time the black Overcome/Passover event. Establish the break with the past, offer the logic for doing things differently and also the interpretive handle for future Overcomings and masteries.

The best thing black liberation can do is to declare that phase one is now over, and that phase two, living the redeemed life, with the massive work of moving beyond the consciousness-raising and describing stage to the building of everything we need from scratch using all our intellect, even the old retired heads in the process, as we build life-saving institutions, other than churches, funeral homes and liquor stores, using to the fullest extent all our collective resources ($204 billion at last count).

Is it because we are still waiting for the Overcoming/Passover (liberating/exalting) event(s) that our song is still blue, our mood stuck in the "shall mode" and our talk grounded only in the pathology of it all? Could it be that black thinkers, preachers and leaders, the change agents and pacesetters in the black communities, are still afraid after all this time to declare Overcome/Passover?

They should have done it through the blackened Jesus. And if He cannot do it, they may indeed need to find the redemptive type elsewhere. I dare remind us that if Jesus cannot become "Christ the Passover sacrificed for

A BLACK PASSOVER

blacks too," then we might need to seize the authority to elevate Martin Luther King, Jr., the only black who could to date be used to signal and mark the Overcome flip for blacks.

The black tradition of asking help of the oppressor, whether by appealing to his (our) common moral sense of right as recorded in the Bill of Rights and our common Bible, or via threats and demands for reparation, such as found in Foreman's Black Manifesto, remains so much like Moses' asking Pharaoh to "Let my people go" in the name of our God. This was nothing short of asking the king to diminish his kingdom of its economically sound labor base, and simply because a magician and a rhetorician asked for it and did a few demonstrations of the magic.

All the redemptive pieces are already in the black experience, even in the language to some degree. I even hear Jesse Jackson saying from time to time "our time has come" for the presidency of the United States with him in the office, of course.

Well, the time has indeed come, but not for individual overcoming and advancement, so much as for corporate advancement. The redemptive pieces are indeed already here, but we lack only one thing, the uniting story. We even have already a Declaration of Black Independence,[15] but it was conditional. As it is so much that we think, say and do.

Cone is right. "Any movement of freedom that is dependent upon the oppressor's support for survival is doomed from the start."

The current agenda, as presented by the black liberation thinkers, seems to be requiring the restructuring of the American society, its values and rules to include the peculiar interests of blacks.

Is black freedom-fighting any more than symbolic of dreams and good for some source material for the best rhetoric from the best orators in the world? "Keep on fighting until freedom comes," says Cone, for we expect at some future time "to achieve liberation for the poor and survival for all." But, what shall be the nature of that Vision Glorious; the picture of that well-won liberation. God himself, through His Christ said, the poor will ever be with us. Poverty has nothing to do with liberation.

THE OVERCOME

The widow with her mite, poor but describing herself as having enough and to spare and share, gave, and in the giving and sharing demonstrated that she would not allow her poverty, legitimate as it was in her case, to trap her in the status of a beggar (not being able to become a giver at any level) for all time. In and through that act, she was transformed from being any other poor widow with a mite, to one we will forever remember and preach about. Alas, seeking the wrong message.

We have wrongly linked poverty and the state of being oppressed in the process and thereby presuppose that the success criteria is somehow the absence of poverty. But, this must be off track and black thinkers need to review it. The white man thinks whether under double jeopardy or not, that he is free and truly liberated. But, anyone going into the hills of Allegheny or the alleys of South Baltimore knows that if these poor whites are liberated, it is not because they are not poor. Their poverty cannot only be seen, it can be felt.

I truly hope that black thinkers will re-think as they seek to develop and project would-be success criteria. And I hope that our Overcoming will never be measured by the total absence of poverty—remembering what Jesus said about the poor being always with us.

I hope that it will somehow be located in our corporate resolve to take care of our individual and corporate futures, through hardship and prosperity, through war and Holocaust if such should ever be experienced after the Overcoming/Passover event.

They should come through future depression and want, singing the triumphant song of thanksgiving for victories won by those who went before, on the one hand, and on the other, vowing, like the Jews of the Holocaust, "never again," all the while developing the necessary covenants, basic rules of life and life-saving institutions through which we guarantee that "never again" will there be a sense of nobodyness; never again a placard declaring and affirming manhood; and never again seeking authenticity from without.

For the very strong bonds we build through covenants, the common and basic rules of sisterhood/brotherhood by which we live, and the institutions through which we learn, work, gain advancement and recognition, stand there always to remind us, like the Pyramids of the great pharaohs, of our "already done" achievements. Those institutions will sustain our pride and our children's pride, while providing jobs at all levels for them and services at all levels for them.

What a Vision Glorious, and it is immediately achievable after the Overcome/Passover of blacks leads them to work cooperatively in rebuilding what was deliberately destroyed by their oppressors.

I part company with Cone when he insists we do not romanticize Dr. King's vision of integration or Malcolm X's emphasis on separation, but seek yet another vision, new and beyond theirs, moving to a future, yet to be described.[16] I happen to believe that both conceptions, Dr. King's integration and Malcolm X's separation (nationalism), must be made to stand together, forever in corrective tension, one with the other.

The "apartness," recommended by Malcolm X as his key expression of the Vision Glorious, has much merit when seen in terms similar to those reflected in the following quotation:

> We have come to see that the church needs to separate from the world every so often. It must carry on its own ceremonies of identification, its own acts of worship and praise when and where there are people of the same conversion, who love the same Lord and march under the same banner. The same applies to a race such as ours. Not in isolation, but in retreat and communion among ourselves we must find our true selves in terms of those shaping events which have formed our peculiar and singular historical experience in this land.[17]

The "apartness or retreat" recommended above and key to the thinking of Malcolm X as he expresses his Vision Glorious for black people has much merit when seen in these terms. For it is not unlike the Jewish decision for the most part to live in updated, modern ghettos, wherever they find themselves in the world. In and through the ghettos they gain strength—political, economic, spiritual, cultural—and they build and sustain all the needed life-saving and supporting institutions.

The scriptures suggest that the "apartness" into which Jesus led His disciples was redemptive, cleansing, creative, restoring, preparatory. He called them apart that they might be empowered. He gave them power and authority. And this separateness can be for good, but it is only one part of the "Vision Glorious." We must find some creative way of bridging the double Vision Glorious as captured by Dr. King and Malcolm X.

Will it be an exclusive glorious ghetto, or a strong cohesive ghetto community from which we gain all the strengths the Jews garnered from their ghetto experiences? Will it be a ghetto community from which we walk into the larger world not as beggars and "under" in any sense of the word, but as strong competent men, ready to make our contributions and receive our rewards, financial, philanthropic and other, to be returned to the ghetto, a reconstituted ghetto, for strength and sustenance?

Our reconstituted ghetto might then look more like a Harlem with redone brownstones worth $1.5 million; or like Pikesville, Maryland. But, it would be home, supported by like folk, with like means and dreams. A haven after a full day of competitive integration in the world of business, education, finance, philanthropy, et al.

All of the above shall happen rather quickly after the enabling experience of the black Overcome/Passover through which those who were once faint-hearted and "under" are reminded that through God's Overcoming event they are now an "over people," and from henceforth as many as would receive this message and be initiated into the Overcome life of black people, such would be given the enabling power to become sons and daughters of the Overcome.

For such would be the only description becoming the black man, the world over, after the declaring of his Overcome/Passover event as an act of Allah/God, in a moment in time (our time too) through the life/ministry/sacrifice/exaltation of Martin Luther King, Jr.

The Jews as an ethnic group have found survival strength in their doing exactly what Malcolm proclaimed. They unified themselves, even living in Jewish plush

A BLACK PASSOVER

ghettos for economic, political and spiritual strength; unifying to build and sustain life-saving institutions and at the same time moving from their new-found suburban ghettos (where they continue to dwell in ghetto community for identity and strength) to the financial, political, artistic and philanthropic centers where they must be reckoned with (a kind of significant integration) precisely because they have learned how to successfully build that nation, within a nation. They have learned the techniques of moving in and out, as warranted, and so should blacks.

Blacks of the Overcome/Passover era must indeed do the same. But, before that can happen, they must make legends about Dr. King and Malcolm X. Like King David, the arch sinner, who turns out in Jewish literature to be the man after God's own heart, who kills 10,000's and overcame Israel's menacing Goliath to become the type of the Messiah, so we owe it to Martin Luther King, Jr. and Malcolm X, to be about the business of re-mythologizing, deliberately building the story, larger than life and inclusive of the redemptive message, to interpret the lives and victories of our leaders.

And since our oppressors like to have us killed when we show strong leadership skills, we need all the more to value mythology. Through this, we can pack the lives of our historical-mythological heroes with all the redemptive positives needed. We can make Malcolm X look like John the Baptist, and Martin Luther King, Jr. look like the peaceful Christ. And we win.

Because myth brings them back to life, the kind of life that can be used for teaching purposes. But, most importantly, they cannot kill them again. And myth has this way of helping us to devalue the peculiar sins and weaknesses of an individual, all in a strategic effort to create a new man. How Pygmalion!

And although I here place Malcolm X and Dr. King together, I dare say that we need to offer redemptive prominence to Dr. King, not because he was indeed any greater or more effective leader than Malcolm X, but simply because both being dead, only one has been elevated and through that elevation had his life and ministry vindicated and lifted up forever and that is Dr. King. And, yet there is a key place for Malcolm X, as we find his significance in the nation-building aspects of our redemption.

The Black Manifesto called for reparations in the amount of $1/2 billion from the white establishment. An honorable request was made in 1969, led by James Foreman.[18] The Black Manifesto, is however, a classic pre-liberation document. It makes a request for the funds; it begs and reasons with the oppressor. He may or he may not respond as requested. The Moses of the pre-liberation times did beg Pharaoh to let his people go. Moses did this at least ten times with ten correlated acts or demonstrations. Then, he declared Passover and walked, and it was the freed people who on the other side of the Red Sea knew that they must use their own jewels to build their own gods of the future.

I have said all this to get to this point. After the Overcoming/Passover event, we do it ourselves. Even with our mites, like the widow Jesus praised, we become givers. Philanthropy beginning with us, and not us as always the recipient of someone's philanthropy.

Should we succeed at making Overcome/Passover a part of the matrix of acceptable conventions; should it become the divider, like the Red Sea in the salvation history of the Israelites, then we can easily place the burden of the 1969 Black Manifesto squarely on our own shoulders. It would require only $16 per black man to reach that goal, our goal.

And it would not entail the begging of any other race for the funds to empower us. And if we do indeed control $204 billion and cannot with all our bright people make it work in our corporate behalf, always using it for the benefit of others, whose fault will that be?

And if we cannot do it now, when? And if not us, then who shall do it? And if we cannot trust each other, not even our Supreme Court justices to watch over our redemptive investment, then we are indeed, poor, black and in real trouble, and forever.

After Overcoming, which in some ways could be as simple as changing the lyrics of the song, "We Shall Overcome Someday," to "We Have Overcome Today," comes the long and tedious work of making dreams real; of turning the "Vision Glorious" into an institutionalized reality.

A BLACK PASSOVER

The Black Manifesto is by no means bad thinking. But, it must be changed from being pre-liberation and "begging" (under) to being post-liberation (over the Red Sea, after the break) and being (giving), recognizing like the widow with the mite, that we have enough and to spare, enough and to share from the standpoint of givers and not beggars.

The logic of reparation, one which called for raising $1/2 billion, though OK, must be reviewed. We might find that now we need $1 billion or more for the empowering work of black institution building. The shift in the logic is located in our recognition that we must now do it ourselves, if we are not to remain forever beggars. A gift of $32 from each black across the country can quickly create the $1 billion endowment fund that could wisely generate thereafter $100 million for yearly development way into the future.

As Cone so correctly points out, "The fight is not just for the acquisition of economic and political rights, but also the establishment of the dignity of black humanity as defined in its cultural past and its current fight for material freedom."[19]

Real dignity will entail that we must do it ourselves. In the contemporary world with all looking on, we should do what Marcus Garvey so nobly attempted, only with a greater sophistication, and with an eye to win, beat the oppressor at his own game.

The major thrust of our talk cannot be directed to whites, either to chide them, to convert them or get them to save us. This time, we must develop, identify and enthrone our own redeemer/savior figure. And our race had better be able to produce one, or else we shall be forced to go outside even for our Santa Claus.

In other words, directing our rhetoric to whites is tantamount to asking them to become our saviors. In a real sense, we have been to the pharaoh far in excess of the permitted ten (10) times with reasonable requests/demands each time. We have demonstrated our power, political power in the marches and in consequent elections, and economic power in bringing down the bus system of Montgomery, Alabama.

We can now accept the fact that we shall get the same "type" of answer every time, whether the black leader be

THE OVERCOME

Moses, Martin Luther King, Jr., or James Foreman of Black Manifesto fame doing the asking.

At the right time, which time is now, we declare the Overcome/Passover event; we assume the total responsibilities for today and our futures; we pool our resources, meagre or otherwise, in order to effect the Black Manifesto in our time and in our children's time.

I often think about the possibility of dying before my people have learned their Passover song. I often think about the older man/woman, with one foot in the grave, who is forced to sing, "We Shall Overcome Someday," as he/she approaches his/her personal end-time, forced because the body of conventions within the black community, to date, grants no permission for our singing so affirmative a song. There are no "Overcome" concepts in the language of our people.

Our Overcome/Passover is our corporate rite of passage, through which we pass, via symbols that are 100 percent authentic to blacks, from being slaves, children, wards of the state or an "under people" in any sense of the concept, to our new found status that describes us as not only free, but also responsible for all aspects of our tomorrow: values, family life, laws, covenants, sense of conscience and shame, with passion for philanthropy. Philanthropy is a key sign of having overcome, for through it all are taught and reminded that each must make significant contributions to the larger human race. What is more, however, is the fact that it is through efforts at philanthropic giving, however small be the gift, that our people will be changed from being 90 percent beggars, always with hand out, to becoming "givers."

Givers, not beggars, even if all there is to give is a mite, a smile or good and wise advice. So, part of the new description we offer ourselves after our break with the past as permission requesters, is that which sees us as givers having enough and to spare and share with the other. And this too will soon become a part of the corporate black culture, what we elsewhere call the informative matrix of concepts and conventions.

The real value of the Overcome rests in its ability to offer a new beginning self-description to black people. To date, our primary descriptions as black point to skin color and not to our character and its quality or content as suggested by Dr. Martin Luther King, Jr. Black, sorry to say, is not a significant description and cannot in and of itself function as a teaching tool in our effort to change our situation. Blacks are everywhere: in high places, low places, in jail and still in the womb. Black is currently a description that is lacking of character traits. There is no saving content resident in the concept...yet. It is a generic term. So too for the matter is African-American. They are everywhere and nowhere at the same time. No character or dispositional traits are implied.

The Overcome offers a new self-description of the character-dispositional sort. It is strategically placed to convey this new self-description. After the Overcome, blacks are to be seen as overcomers by nature. They are that by birth (right and rite) and by definition. The meaning: they will henceforth overcome any and all trials and tribulations placed in their way. We know this because our forebears overcame much worse predicaments. In and through the repeated successful overcoming of perplexities, they have forged for us a new character, the character of the overcomer. They expect us on their suffering and on their blood to re-describe ourselves as overcomers and go on to overcome any, every, and all perplexities, personal or societal in our futures.

Black theology becomes central to our thinking only because it claims to be a theology of liberation. The National Committee on Black Churchmen's Black Theology statements of June 13, 1969 said:

> Black theology is a theology of liberation. It seeks to plumb the black condition in the light of God's revelation in Jesus Christ, so that the black community can see that the Gospel of Jesus is commensurate with the achievement of black humanity.[20]

The presupposition here is that black humanity is an achievement that comes only after some relevant struggle, a process of some sort through which black people become human. This is without doubt the kind of flawed thinking that informs a people in a way that keeps them in a "hoping," "shalling" mood, stuck in what I call the pre-liberation mood. The fact of the matter is that black humanity is not an achievement granted after any successful struggle. Black humanity is a "given" that comes with birth, and nothing done to it can take away its intrinsic God-given humanity.

But, our theological, philosophical, sociological and psychological starting points remain so flawed that we remain trapped conceptually, linguistically and psychologically in the process-evolutionary way of looking at ourselves.

The Genesis descriptive story is not about evolution or process. God spake and it was done; He described it (creation and man within it) as good, and it was good. There is a process. But capable and competent people with a corporate character, the Overcome character, are on the pilgrim's road, and not some things or somebodies that become at the end of the journey.

So, the point must be made again until it is registered. Our humanity is not gained after any struggle or process. It is the beginning "given."

Yes, even today and in black liberation thinking, something must stand as a given and not up for debate or argument. Historical starting points have this way of trapping us into process-like understandings about ourselves. And unless we can start the history (like Bible) somewhere in pristine formative mythology and emerge from that into valid interpretations of the facts of history, the bare facts of black history in America can indeed lead one to draw despairing conclusions about the past and prospects for the future.

But there is another way.

The greatness of the Greeks, what keeps them proud, is hardly their bare history. It is more the pristine myths about heroes and gods and former glorious times. It works. We know what they are doing. The results are efficacious. Whenever we are inclined to adopt the thinking that blacks need to achieve humanity through Jesus or anybody else, we need to raise the red flag. We were already human. Christ died for us as brothers/sisters and joint/fellow heirs of the kingdom.

Should notions like these become part of the staple diet being fed black Christians by their most revered pastors, we are indeed "poor, black and in trouble."

A BLACK PASSOVER

Rather, remember that black humanity is nothing less than a given from God which no set of circumstances, humiliation, conquering or enslaving can negate. This must be true even from Christian standpoints, because Jesus was indeed humiliated and done-in.

But, that at no stage made him any less the son of God. We can never be "not human" now and "human" later. Until this gets imbedded in the thoughts of our people, that their humanity even in the midst of poverty, slavery and want is not essentially negated, one of the key presuppositions, a recurring thought in the writings of even a man of the calibre of James Cone, will remain flawed and dysfunctional to the achievement of the very end, the strategic aims of the intellectual exercise in liberation.

I beg to remind us all, however, that the absence of racism cannot be the primary evidence we seek for claiming the arrival of the Overcome/Passover event. Like the poor who shall be ever with us, racism, bigotry and pre-judging of one sort or another will forever be with us.

Should our Vision Glorious, our picture of the land flowing with milk and honey be reduced to a picture wherein there is an absence of racism, we will in that one action guarantee the delay of the arrival of Overcome/Passover forever.

Cone's certainty that the key Biblical liberation paradigm could be located in the Exodus story is on target and key to his own theology. He says: "God's call of his people (Israel) is related to their oppressed condition and his own liberating activity already seen in the Exodus. You have seen what I did. By delivering his people from Egyptian bondage and inaugurating the covenant on the basis of that historical event, God reveals that He is the God of the oppressed, involved in their history, liberating them from human bondage."[21]

Cone's claim has point in the pre-liberation state, while we are yet oppressed. God is indeed forever on the side of the oppressed. Does it mean that we should forever stay in that state to guarantee God's favor and stance? And what would happen if we were no longer the oppressed? Where would God stand in relation to us?

Cone is missing the key point, the redemptive lesson that the Exodus experience teaches. For the grammar or logic of the Exodus liberating event was neither a statement of recognition about what Moses accomplished in God's name nor what God did for Israel through Moses.

The simple declaration of God being on the side of the oppressed is not where the significance of Exodus is to be found.

Rather, the Exodus was the walking into freedom (the redemptive activity) that was the consequence of the spiritual, mental, and psychological Passover, its corollary that was first demonstrated through the rite of spilled blood (lambs) and consummated in the triumphant walk, a walk across the sea. All our attempts to use the Exodus story to confirm us in our "on-going struggle" is exactly where the paradigm of the Exodus will always and forever fail us.

The Exodus is *not* the struggle, it is not the trying. Rather it is the triumphant, climaxing walk, the first in a never-ending series of liberating activities done in the "Passover mood," after the recognition that the pre-liberation stance of Moses, one in which he used various forms of persuasion, even magical and destructive demonstrations through the 10 plagues to gain the liberation of his people had failed; after recognizing that a truly liberated people do not ask for permission—they are no longer beggars, but people who though poor and initially without money, education or institutions, dare to take their future into their hands and walk.

A BLACK PASSOVER

Notes for Chapter Four

[1] Manos Buthelezi, cited in Wilmore/Cone, Black Theology, p. 232.

[2] An excerpt from the Address of Joseph A. Johnson, Bishop of the Fourth Episcopal District of the C.M.E. Church, held in Memphis, Tenn., 1970. Cited in Wilmore/Cone, Black Theology, p. 280.

[3] Ibid. p. 281.

[4] Edward R. Braxton, in Wilmore/Cone, Black Theology, pp. 325-327.

[5] Black Theology, p. 245.

[6] Ibid, p. 224.

[7] Ibid, p. 224.

[8] Ibid, p. 230.

[9] Ibid, p. 224.

[10] Ibid, p. 230.

[11] Ibid, p. 230.

[12] Ibid, pp. 220 ff.

[13] "The Black Paper." Statement by Black Methodists for Church Renewal. Cited in: Wilmore/Cone Black Theology, pp. 268 ff.

[14] Ibid, p. 269.

[15] "The Black Declaration of Independence," July 4, 1970. Cited in Wilmore/Cone, Black Theology, pp. 108-111.

[16] James H. Cone. "For My People." New York: Orbis Books. 1984. pp. 190 ff..

[17] "President's Message to the Progressive National Baptist Convention, Inc., September, 1968. Cited in Wilmore/Cone, Black Theology, p. 265.

[18] "The Black Manifesto." Cited in Wilmore/Cone Ibid pp. 80-89.

[19] Cone, "For My People," p. 47.

[20] "Statement by National Committee of Black Churchmen," June 13, 1969. Cited in Wilmore/Cone, Black Theology, p. 101.

[21] James H. Cone. "A Black Theology of Liberation." Philadelphia and New York: J. D. Lippincott Co. 1970. p. 18.

Chapter Five

Dr. King's Death And Elevation: The Symbol of the Overcome

Black theologians claimed that God is on the side of the oppressed. This claim was strongly held by them, much to the chagrin of many a white theologian who just knew that God could not do that—take the side of blacks—but was a God concerned with sin and disobedience. Sin, white or black, and sin, whether it was related to the ravages associated with slavery, oppression or whatever.

The Old Testament actually has God using oppressors to chastise his wayward people, and so the Persian invader-kings were often seen, not always as oppressors, but as chosen vessels of God to chasten a sinful nation.

But black theologians speak as though there is no sin in the black community that God may be punishing. What about the sins connected with the "crab in the basket" syndrome that embodies the disobedience to the Tenth Commandment enjoining against covetous behaviors?

Should black leaders face the sin in the black community, they would need to respond to William Jones's query raised in his most challenging book, *Is God a White Racist?* [1]

There he raised the challenge for black theologians that this work attempts to answer: If God is on the side of blacks as most black theologians love to claim, if he is about liberating them from their oppression and poverty, where is the liberating/authenticating/exalting event that one can point to in order to substantiate that claim?

Jones hints that the overwhelming evidence is on the other side, and that one could as easily conclude that God is a white racist, divinely hurting and punishing blacks. His concept about the multi-evidentiality[2] of the claims and counter claims sets the stage for his forceful argument which must yet be addressed.

In this work, we offer two choices. We must either stop questioning the once-for-all-time efficacy of the Overcoming, triumphant event entailed in the Christ story; accept it as that liberating event, and claim the resulting victory so that we can go on from this point. Or, we must offer another event, peculiar for us and resident in Martin Luther King, Jr.

But, there may be a third option (functional at least on the cultural, psychological and political levels) whereby we accept the primacy of the once for all time efficacy of the Christian Overcoming/Passover event. An event good for all people while deliberately developing a language that can say effectively that God is, through the life, death and elevation of Martin Luther King, Jr., reminding us, in a pictorial and forceful way, of that which has already been done on the religious plane.

It is finished and complete and of the political/cultural psychological Overcoming that is to be declared and gained through the proper interpretation of the events around the life, death and elevation of our own liberator type (political, psychological and cultural). It then becomes a kind of sermon that is there to remind us and force upon us the peculiarity of our own existence.

Dr. King never did claim to be anything other than a humble Christian minister, an agent doing his part of the redemptive work. But, he may still be God's gift to us to wrought, once and for all time, a political, economic, cultural and psychological Overcoming/Passover event that will work in setting the break between the "before" and "after" of our historical development.

I will not advocate here any new religion with any new Christ. Such would not help. It will only further fragmentalize, and at a time when we need a uniting, not a dividing story. A new religion would only offer us another "ism" to further divide us. But, a language could be developed to facilitate the making of Dr. King's peculiar status—equal to that of the great father of America, George Washington—and Christian to the very core, significant in the total redemptive plan of God.

William Jones had his finger squarely on the main issue. Before the claims made by black liberation theologians can be authenticated, some primary and bold claim must be made and generally accepted as to the locale of God's redemptive and vindicating act,[3] as peculiar to blacks. I am, myself, personally convinced that Dr. King's real and abiding significance, his eternal value, his redemptive contribution to the blacks of the world for whom he lived and died, is located somewhere in this scheme of thought. And that better minds ought to get busy developing the interpretive story (myth) to be told over and over again.

Can anyone think of another person; another set of circumstances or events? The aspect of elevation (much like resurrection, Passover, Overcome) is present. The elevation to the same status as George Washington just about guarantees certain immortality. Most telling in the choosing of Dr. King as the lamb for the black political/cultural/psychological Overcoming/Passover is that he was a Baptist preacher from the most independent peculiarly black tradition of religion in the south.

If God is the liberator on the side of blacks and the oppressed, His servant, Dr. King, did something very significant in His service, something far more significant than what is currently pointed to. Martin Luther King, Jr. offered more than a dream or vision. Dreams and visions are airy and ghost-like; they can evaporate from memory if not incorporated and installed in the corpus of conventions and kept alive through institutional life.

What Dr. King achieved for us, and on our behalf, was the final elevation of former slaves from the negative status of second class citizenship to the new status. The God-like aspects to this event are resident in the fact that this new status was assigned and installed, once and for all time, with the pen and signature of President Ronald Wilson Reagan, a man considered by blacks across the country to be most against their interests in recent years. Like Lincoln, however, Reagan has already done the most significant thing for blacks during this century and roughly 100 years after Lincoln signed the emancipation act.

Blacks in America have now gained symbolic parity. And that is all a government like ours can do.

We are capitalist and governed by law. We are rewarded for our personal achievements. The rest is in our hands. For the context has been set for introducing our Overcoming/Passover song, "We Have Overcome Today."

If we cannot even now sing that song, then God has indeed failed us as liberator, or we have failed to recognize his liberating act.

In either case, we are doomed because we must claim his redemptive act before moving into the redeemed future. And the inability to do this, for whatever reason, will have the net result of forever locking black thinkers into raising redemptive questions which will never be answered.

William R. Jones criticizes Joseph Washington's view that the black experience of suffering, the total pathological plight black people find themselves in, is comparable to the "suffering servant" typology of the Bible.[4] Washington thinks that the suffering should be thus viewed, managed and interpreted, and so blacks in America are seen by Washington as God's contemporary suffering servants. Jones points to flaws in Washington's work by reminding all that apart from an identification of the black liberating/exalting event, Washington's arguments cannot stand. Jones refers to Washington's theory of blacks as the contemporary suffering servants of God as "a mythical hope with precious little relationship to reality."[5]

As far as Jones is concerned, any legitimate likening of the black experience of peculiar ethnic suffering to the type of the suffering servant of the Jewish scriptures must be accompanied by the "identification of the requisite liberation/exaltation event which is indispensable for the Biblical model of the suffering servant."[6]

Jones agrees with the argument that using the Biblical model as the interpretive handle for managing contemporary black pathology is attractive but inadequate. This is precisely because such a paradigm does not jibe with the actual experience of blacks to this date. They have not yet been able to identify that liberation exaltation event through which the servant is vindicated, made in a real sense to overcome his suffering with the help of his God.

Washington recognizes this need for an exaltation event that validates liberation from suffering because he points to the Resurrection of Jesus: "The Resurrection is the sequel to the cross. Without Easter morning, Good Friday would be bad Friday, for evil would have the last word."[7]

Jones thinks that Washington wants to postpone the liberation/exaltation event for sometime in the future, some eschatological event. Again Jones reminds us that a future liberation/exaltation event cannot count, since it is not normal to "categorize suffering as vicarious prior to the exaltation event. Suffering as vicarious is more given to be a retrospective determination."[8]

Jones is correct in his analysis. The lead song of black liberation movements, of most liberation movements the world over, is "We Shall Overcome Someday." These words connote a hope for the future, implicitly saying that the liberation/exaltation event has not yet arrived, cannot yet be identified, not even as a foretaste.

I believe that the black liberation thinkers must, before moving into the future, before claiming the special privilege status as God's suffering servants, move to identify the Overcoming/Passover event. The black theologian is somehow aware of this requirement, and I believe that was what motivated them first to paint God black, and later God's Christ, Jesus, the redemptive prototype, black.

But, a generation after making Jesus and God, His Father, black, not much has changed either in the language or the perception of black liberation thinkers.

The time might be here for the introduction of a rather radical notion. A notion that forces the consideration of the Overcoming/Passover event on blacks, in the person of Martin Luther King, Jr., whose life, ministry, death and exaltation, offers a striking type of the redemptive event required by blacks if they are truly to establish the interpretive page break.

A page break that depicts the "before" and "after" of

blacks' existence, and so sets the stage for managing not only the interpretation of their pathological American historical experience, but through that event find a way to overcome it psychologically, with ritual and rite and then move boldly into the future.

The Jews of old made and declared their Passover,[9] not even via the death of their Moses; Moses being smart enough to devise a ritual of blood using lamb's blood as the symbol and sign of the arrival of the Overcome event. Jews made and declared Passover, and experienced their liberating/exalting event with the passage through the Red Sea. Blacks have a dynamite event in their very contemporary experience that needs to be interpreted and used with effect, the effect of Overcoming the paralysis of futurism, future deliverance, when they have in reality what the Jews had to create, and 5,000 years ago, while, slaves, and not 400 years after emancipation.

Discovering the liberating/exaltating event in the life, ministry, death and elevation of Martin Luther King, Jr. cannot be beat. For one, he is dead already, killed—they can't kill him again; he is already exalted; no other black (or white) for that matter will be elevated in the foreseeable future. He is perhaps the only Christ-type available to blacks, through whom could be established the much-needed, required liberation/exaltation event.

Archbishop Desmund Tutu, of South Africa, has been offered as an alternative, but he is not "martyred" yet; tears have not been shed for his blood as yet, and no myths about his saving value have yet been established. And he has not been exalted quite like Dr. King, yet.

Black liberation thinkers continue to react to whites' resistance to the introduction, not of color, but black color, into the Christological arena. The black theologian was declaring, through this act, with confidence, the blackness of Jesus.

Battle lines were drawn. It was at this point that I became interested in Black Liberation Theology and black liberation as done in the American key. As a student at the Yale Divinity School back in the early 1970's, students, white and black, were treated to a stirring lecture about the blackness of Jesus (as the fact of the matter as far as the speaker was concerned).

After the lecture, one white student, male and friend

of mine, turned to me and said in a simple, matter of fact manner, "I couldn't deal with a black Jesus." That was the end of the matter as far as he was concerned. I could no longer sit on the fence and pretend that there was no issue here. I have never forgotten that and never could. If he could not deal with a black redeemer, could not even grant another the option to thus conceptualize his redeemer, what was I doing dealing with all those real images that made Jesus white and blue-eyed.

Then came my reflections on Santa Claus and Father Christmas, the only person in the world who graciously gave and in the dead of night, in an effort to guarantee that he would not even gain thanks for his special undeserved kindness, and certainly, no reward. He remained nice and white, thrown at my people to the point at which I have seen black children crying and refusing to go to the black Santa Claus in shopping malls at Christmas.

The same child will go to the white Santa, take a present and a picture. What does that do to the black father and mother who are often the real Santas? What lunacy! We do have a problem, psychological, linguistic and existential.

I suspect that these concerns, and others, are of the nature of what informed and framed the thinking of black liberation thinkers into dealing with racism as the central issue in black liberation talk.

But, this is a great mistake. Black liberation thinkers seem to be hoping for the day when they will be truly accepted by whites, walking hand in hand. And, they want to walk hand in hand with whites before they learn to walk hand in hand with each other. Sometimes when I listen to the hymn, "We Shall Overcome Someday," I wonder what is the nature of that Overcoming. And, the desire to walk hand in hand, if taken to mean with whites everywhere, is part of a Vision Glorious that can only further delay the moment when Overcoming can be declared. "Hand in hand" with each other, though as difficult a task in the current world of black diversity and division at all levels, would be a better vision, at the first stage.

The failure of whites to allow integration (sought by blacks in schools, neighborhoods and resisted by whites consistently) demonstrates that whites for the most part have no intention of aiding any such Vision Glorious. Blacks love to follow whites into their communities, even when this means leaving their former communities without role models, without resources to beautify.

This writer sees white resistance to black integration at this pre-liberation stage as a key blessing from God, designed to give us time to declare our Overcome/Passover and claim what is already ours, as heirs to all that is God's.

The most amazing thing to witness in the black community is that despite the fact that many blacks have all the trappings of success, the money, sophistication, real estate, education, etc.; even when they own successful businesses, key jobs; even if they are members of Congress making top dollar and wielding immense power, wanting for nothing, they still believe and talk and act in an under mode. They will sing the blues; and they talk without triumph. In the black community, it is a cardinal sin to boast about successes and personal achievement.

The consequence is one in which we have communities devoid of people who dare to boast of their successes that others can see and find a way of overcoming. And so, we see our liberation thinkers would have us to continue believing that the centerpiece of the liberation effort is the fight against racism. So, they keep racism as the central theme and focus of their thinking and writing.

This writer believes that keeping racism as the strategic aim of Dr. King and others is nothing more than an exercise at dreaming the impossible dream at this stage of the game. Whites in their right minds would not want to integrate with a people who hate themselves, a people with no life-saving institutions, nothing to trade.

They will continue to take the cream of the crop and offer them special status. But, the vast majority will remain on the fringes until peoplehood is established with the advent of the black Overcome/Passover equalizing event, with its correlated efforts at establishing institutions that offer what others need to acquire.

In others words, there will never be in our lifetime any true redemption from racism or classism. If such is that we seek, we have failed before getting started. A clarification of the picture of the Vision Glorious is what we need at this stage of the game. And this must happen now if our song of hope shall not be forever, "We Shall Overcome Someday."

I long to hear the song, "We Have Overcome Today," take its place as the lead song in the Overcome/Passover event, not just because I want to advocate the change in the lyrics of a song, but because I am absolutely convinced that for a people stuck in a morbid history like blacks—trapped in a language of the blues—with a body of conventions that contains few if any victories or successes that can be corporately celebrated, a once-for-all time Overcoming/Passover event is required.

Simply claiming that Jesus is black would not do it either. Black theologians made both God and Jesus black and still sang the pre-liberation song. It did not do it. It can, however, help to set the stage. I have already received Christmas cards from Chinese and Indian friends who send the Madonna and Child represented in their image of their best-looking Chinese or Indian mother and child. That needed no argument. Only in the black community is a question about the authority to so represent Madonna and Child raised.

We need to become like the Chinese and Indians in this regard and get to the stage where we can naturally and with ease consider it appropriate to thus represent the perfect mother and the sacrificial son.

For if God could not have chosen my dear black mother as the Madonna, if that option is not even available to us, we are indeed outside the pale of His redemptive reach.

It should be obvious that the blackness of Jesus, as declared by some black theologians, was long overdue. But, it is not in and of itself redemptive.

However, if on claiming blackness for Jesus, at least as an option for black people, the stage has been set on which the once-for-all-time redemptive act of God, through the Christ-type, (here the black Jesus), effected in a truly efficacious way the Overcoming/Passover of us all, then black Christians ought to become truly exultant and triumphant and with some ease change their pre-liberation song, "We Shall Overcome Someday," to a song that reflects that "We Have Already Overcome" because we share in the redemptive victory wrought by that "black Christ" of black liberation theology.

Or, did black theologians just "say" it, thinking that in the saying of a thing is the doing of the thing? Did they not truly understand its Overcoming/Passover import, with its transforming characteristics?

If we are to take black theologians at their word and accept that for black Christians the Messiah, Jesus, was indeed black, and wrought our redemption as part of God's providential plan of being on the side of the oppressed and winning victories for them, then it is indeed time that we exult and become triumphant, knowing that we have overcome in the Lord and through the lives of countless saints and prophets, the trailblazers who went before, preparing the way for us.

And, we should begin to think, hope, intend, live and act in the key of an Overcoming people. I wait and pray for this actuality, knowing full well that apart from the declaration of our having overcome, our lives, our writings, our poems, our hopings, our intendings and our doings will always be and forever be in the "shall mode."

And worse, we shall die in that mode, singing or having sung on our behalf, "We Shall Overcome Someday." A lie for Christians.

For their theology declares that they have already overcome in their Jesus. That is the message of Easter...Christ our Passover is sacrificed for us, therefore let us keep the feast.[10] The Easter hymn says it also, "The strife is oe'r, the battle done,...the victory won...the song of triumph hath begun...alleluya."

My plea is one that begs of blacks that they introduce into their thinking a real sense of triumphalism, around the redemptive work of Jesus (the black Jesus, if they can really accept a black Jesus as an option and good for them) and around the life, death and elevated vindication of Martin Luther King, Jr. for all blacks, Christian, Muslim, Rastafarians[11] and other.

How about some of that triumphalism that the white Christians have developed out of the same Christian story, from the same Bible, and to such precision that in the Episcopal Church, where I find my place as priest, triumphalism is precisely what many theologians and thinking priests are attacking. They think that they have

A BLACK PASSOVER

too much of it. Black Christians, on the other hand, have none or much too little. And triumphalism is indeed part of the Christian story.

It is Easter and every Sunday. We do need to introduce some triumphalism into the corpus of conventions that form and govern black lives, never forgetting paradox as central to existence and never forgetting the "now and not yet" aspects of any redemptive or liberative exercise.

As hinted above, for non-Christian blacks, another event must become that through which we all, blacks, can declare, proclaim and share in the celebration of this liberating Overcoming/Passover event.

In this regard, I dare to remind us that Dr. King and his sacrificial life, death and elevation—with the appropriate myth or larger than life stories that will posit him as our one suffering servant—whose redemptive work in and our behalf (what he lived and died for)—has now been vindicated, lifted up and exalted by all, blacks and whites alike, can work for us. In his possible story (myth) could be located all the ingredients appropriate to the one who for blacks can fix the redemptive language, getting us beyond the pre-liberation stage to the liberation stage when we discover that we have a "done deal."

We must now in earnest move on and start building all the life-saving institutions, from stable families to hospitals and Fortune 500 companies that we shall need to keep us in the new-found Overcome status.

Martin Luther King, Jr. must be seen as the chosen one. He suffered for his people worldwide, and he has now been vindicated and exalted. He must be chosen in the first stage effort of coalescing blacks into a (one) people with a common something—redemptive story.

As we dare to build the myth, the interpretive story that would fit our redemptive personality and our redemptive event—even if "somebodies" would dare to attack the person and the event (as they surely will), as we tell the story, as it is taught to our children and our children's children—we must forever and always know what we are doing.

We are identifying and installing the locale of our peculiar salvation event. To separate this from religion and the centrality of Jesus for Christians, we might need to see this as the political/nation-building side of the redemptive event.

In this sense, all blacks could participate without creating another "ism" that could divide, further delaying the coming together that is needed by black peoples. Therefore, in identifying the locale of our salvation event, in dating it, in developing its rites and appropriate rituals and its interpretive myth about its timeless value to us as a people, we accomplish that which has been lacking in the evolution of recent black thinking.

We introduce triumph. We introduce celebration and new beginning in the key whereby we accept the full and total responsibility, individually and corporately for our futures. And with that acceptance, we go about the difficult task of destroying all that frustrates our goals, and put in its place all that will enhance them. Challenge to will, to persevere and to effect, will be the hallmark of the new age.

In this process, we are simply reminding ourselves that suffering, pain, bad experiences, can never be overcome as a people (corporately) until the body corporate can identify and justify the event (real or contrived) through which that which was broken down and neglected has been lifted up.

And it will never and can never mean that each and every member of the newly redeemed race has already arrived or is saved. Some will yet be poor, many will still be in prison, many more will fail, or refuse to understand and accept the strategic move of declaring Overcome/Passover. Nothing is new here. So did the murmurers and dissenters in Moses' day. Such must be left behind.

"They will soon come bringing their tails behind them." In the meantime, their objections and arguments against Overcoming/Passover can be used to force the redeemed corpus to fine tune its thinking, correct its errors, and set timetables for institutional-building to prove that it was right. A page break must be made with the past, a past in which we were dependent, and always asking permission, allowing others to set standards of valuing, to establish beauty and success criteria for us.

This is a time when we take our present and future totally into our own hands; to rise or fall because of our choices and decisions; and to out-think, out-fox and fight when and where and how necessary to maintain our control over the life-saving institutions which we build as an Overcoming/Passover people.

In order to ready ourselves for these tasks, it will be required of us that we date the moment of change, and so introduce into our thinking the before/after interpretive handle.

The work ahead, after this declaration of the black Overcome/Passover event, will be overwhelmingly challenging. It could be frightening and frighten blacks into denying the need to make this move. For we are talking about a new beginning in a new mood and key. Everything must be re-described. Everything must be seen through the spectacles of an Overcome black people.

God has given us, in these days, that victorious, validating person and the liberating exaltation event to go along with him. This is without doubt the age and the moment to work the wonder as we become active participants in the shaping of the interpretation of our history and experiencing a redemptive way, for ourselves and for our children's children. And, we need not forever appropriate the redemptive experiences of others (especially if we cannot make them truly work to bring about the redemptive end, even after many centuries of trying and after many creative adaptations) when in our midst, as gift from God, a redemptive type is present and very much alive in the memory of blacks the world over.

More, many of us who are now living actively participated in the evolution of this redemptive political event. Many marched in demonstrations asking through those marches with Dr. King for permission to let God's people go to be and to become. Many were imprisoned, beaten; some were killed, the first martyrs of the final redemptive event. But then, the blood of the chosen one, Dr. King, was spilled, and this one was later elevated with the help of people I know personally, people I have preached to and touched.

And, if we do not want to wait another century or more for the rise of another MLK-type, whose work may never again be vindicated and elevated, we had better agree on the recurring thesis of this book. Dr. King cannot be killed again. And our children need not die, when one has already died for us.

There is a sense in which those who walked with Dr. King, talked with him, fed him, loved him and touched him; those who taught him, sustained him in his life and work, elevated him after death, are all connected in this once-for-all-time redemptive initial work.

In a real sense, all blacks must be made to participate and share, even if by extension, in the redemptive work of Dr. King. There must become a time, after the process of myth-building, after the fine-tuning of the story, when it is set and complete, having become the "given" and accepted as the given uniting story, when there will be no sense in which blacks, those who went before and those who came after, will not be made true participants, whether by birth or by ritual and rite, in the once and for all time Overcome/Passover event wrought for us in and through the one God chose and the one we accept.

Accepting Martin Luther King, Jr. as the primary and special, if not the only redemptive personality, will be difficult if not impossible for black Christians. Jesus has that prime place. The problem is that even now, as evidenced in the writings and preaching of black Christians, Jesus' redeeming work has not been made to truly work efficaciously in the liberation of blacks who will not with ease learn the new song advocated in this book as the sign of the black Overcoming/Passover event.

The push to find a redemptive place for Dr. King that could be sufficiently foundational to include not only black Christians, but also Muslims, Rastafarians and others, in some uniting/redemptive way of looking at life, must still be made.

And, it is here that I must once more introduce the political way of handling Martin Luther King's Overcome/Passover event, so that it does not conflict with the deep convictions of black Christians, and itself become dysfunctional to the task at hand—uniting us into a people with a story of redemption that meets at least at one point that we can identify, locate and date, and accept as a given whether we are Rastafarians, Christians, Muslims or other.

There is a pattern in our history of identifying Martin Luther King, Jr., as a type of Moses, the liberator. I would

A BLACK PASSOVER

like to pick up this theme once more as I do an analysis of the type of freedom and liberation Moses actually designed, comparing it with that of Dr. King, and in that process demonstrate once more our need for the proclaiming, celebrating and instituting of our Overcome/Passover event, and like Moses and the children of Israel, even the murmurers and detractors, walk corporately into our prosperous futures, much like the Jews, building moral codes, covenants and life-saving/sustaining institutions, which can in time create the true connectedness, one to another, wherever we may find ourselves in the world, whatever our existential circumstances, religion, or current political status.

This, I believe must come first, and with a God-given like quality (not up for questioning at that level) that focuses our unity and resolve to win at whatever we put our hands to, even if the story behind the unity is mythical[12] (true for strategic purposes) like King Arthur's Roundtable or the once-for-all-time crossing of the Red Sea.

The latter analogy captures for us the importance of establishing that story that begins the re-interpretation of our salvation history, with our salvation being won at some level through the efforts and blood of one of our own.

There is that sense in which the experience of blacks in America, and Jews in Africa, as slaves, runs parallel. Of course, the Jews as slaves in Africa were held captive by black men. We placed burdens on them too hard to bear. If you don't believe me, check out the mummies of the African Pharaohs for blackness. We once enslaved others, the Jews for sure. In any event, Jews and blacks were both slaves, though at different times in history.

They were held captives for roughly the same period of time, 400 years, long enough to strip them of their cultural identity, language and self-respect. This was long enough to make them turn over to their oppressors any of their number who went out of line.

They were both made to build vast empires, with structures that stand to this day. Some were raised up as overseers and not only snitched on their brothers, but often proved as difficult a taskmaster as the other could be. Moses had to run to Midian when in his enthusiasm he killed an Egyptian who was brutalizing an Israelite, hoping through this act to endear himself to his fellow Israelite by presenting himself as a defender of the peace, a peacemaker. It backfired.

The solidarity with the brothers Moses sought backfired. Read Exodus for the story. He was later, not only rebuffed, but needed to flee to Midian for his personal safety. Black men are being killed, put in jails and in other ways effectively taken out of the society, much as was done to the first-born males of Israelite slavery days.

The basics of the situations are very similar indeed. But Moses, after his period of self-exile when he met the no-name God, the one who would become what he would become in time and in relationship, returned boldly to Egypt to confront the Pharaoh. He asked permission of the Pharaoh at least 10 times, with the Pharaoh in the end always saying an effective "no," and with Moses doing with increasing intensity his various demonstrations (plagues). It did not work for Moses.

It does not now work for black Americans or blacks the world over. We ask permission. Like Moses, we do miraculous demonstrations of our power and resolve—the March on Washington was nothing short of a miracle. We make immortal speeches, as did Dr. King: "I Have a Dream." And, here ends the analogy. Moses, after 10 askings for permission and 10 demonstrations of power and resolve, never did return to the Pharaoh.

He stopped begging, stopped asking for permission, stopped reasoning and debating with them. He returned to his people and created a simple though effective Passover ceremony of spilled blood—the ceremony of accomplishment, the ceremony of resolve, the ceremony that carries the "never again" such humiliation theme.

And, with and through this simple Passover event, that one act of salvation history, the slaves became former slaves, garnered strength that they always had, but never thought they had the authority to harness to their own benefit, and they walked.

As they walked, they were prepared to make their own gods (first from silver and gold), an act through which they effectually broke with the value system being left behind.

A BLACK PASSOVER

A little reflection will show us that they did this while they were yet slaves and not 125 years after economic conditions forced the captors to dismantle slavery (with its burdensome responsibility of feeding all those families who could no longer under changed economic circumstances truly earn their keep). They left with the resolve that they would overcome as they had already done in Egypt, every and any obstacle to their fully achieving their Vision Glorious of a promised land, filled with milk and honey. They would leave, and through the act of leaving commit themselves to conquer (overcome) all obstacles ahead.

These proved to be many for a truly primitive band of people, with no political system, no economic power, no institutions at this level, but one, a Passover only days old. But, with their new-found God, a God with no name (who will be what He will be and become what He will become as they walk into their future with Him); with their charismatic leader, their Passover and covenant between themselves and their God, they walked into their future.

There would be future rivalry for power. There would be fears. There would be the testing of the god and the making of others from gold and silver, appropriated from their masters in Egypt at the command of Moses (Exodus 12:35-36). They would forever debate different ways of doing this or that, of being inclusive or exclusive (to integrate or not), but they always remained connected in and through the Passover event and the later covenant.

These events saw them through many perplexities, as the history of the Israelites details. It even saw them through the Holocaust of our day and time. Somehow that first Overcoming/Passover event, concocted by Moses, establishing the before and after of dependency and self-reliance, an event from which each age could look back to or forward from; and through which they could be made to vicariously participate in, and know and experience the "already accomplishedness" of the victory over negative forces—gave them strength to do many Overcomings over their long history. Look at the Jewish people now. Check the jails and compare.

Ask a Jew who survived the Holocaust how he could dare to celebrate "Passover" in that existentially powerless situation. In a situation without hope, ripe for despair and suicide, many did Passover. It is in the contemplation of this event that the redemptive necessity for the black Overcome/Passover event is brought to the surface as an issue that must be dealt with, once and for all time, establishing the needed separation in eras (before/after) before blacks can go on.

In the contemplation of the true and abiding significance of Overcome/Passover event, we may discover why modern day Jews (white for the most part) dared to fly incognito into the heart of Ethiopia, in war time, to bring out in succession as many of their black Jewish brothers and sisters as would come. Passover, covenant and brotherly solidarity, when it counts.

Check further and discover how, together, Jews of the American Diaspora have methodically built, maintained and supported every life-saving institution from hospitals to banks; how they survived ghettos, the term coined for them; how they built a nation with the help of the two nations that once discriminated against them, Britain and the America; how they can continue to influence world affairs, military, economic and other, gaining the ear of presidents who continue to treat blacks, a people who outnumber Jews in the America by 30,000,00, with benign neglect.

Our black liberation scholars who have sought paradigms of liberation have skirted or overlooked the key element in liberation, even when viewing Moses and his liberation efforts.

That missed element is all that is truly lacking in the completion of the first stages. If we are ever to move from the pre-liberation stance to the status of liberation, we must also identify/declare/proclaim/celebrate our Overcoming/Passover event. This must be popularly accepted and incorporated into the corpus of the conventions that guide black life. An appropriate "same" ceremony must be developed and done at the same time yearly by all who buy into the concept of the Overcoming/Passover event. It will need "same words" same symbols, same context.

I happen to believe that April 4, 1968 should be named Black Overcome Day. It was the day on which Martin Luther King, Jr. was sacrificed for blacks. There was a time when we talked about his assassination. But, after his vindication and elevation, that word is no longer appropriate. If rats and rabbits in research labs are "sacrificed" and never just simply killed for us, certainly, the same logic can be used in interpreting the life, ministry, death and elevation of Dr. King.

In 1988, a very strange thing happened as I was developing the manuscript for this book. Passover, Easter and Overcome (April 4th) followed each other in perfect sequence.

Chapter Five Notes

[1] William R. Jones. *Is God a White Racist?* (Garden City: Anchor Press/Doubleday, 1973).

[2] Ibid., p. 7.

[3] Ibid., p. 82.

[4] Joseph Washington. *The Politics of God.* Boston: Beacon Press, 1969. pp. 155ff.

[5] Jones. Ibid., pp. 79-80.

[6] Ibid., p. 80.

[7] Washington. Ibid, p. 146.

[8] Jones. Ibid, p. 181.

[9] The Bible, The Book of Exodus.

[10] I Corinthians 5: 708. This passage can help to illuminate the bridge-like aspects of Overcome/Passover from the old way of being, seeing and doing to the new more enlightened and empowered status with its correlated new ways of seeing, doing, hoping and intending, what I call the Overcoming conceptual flip.

[11] It is so revealing to see pictures of Dr. King with guards dressed like Muslims, surrounding and protecting him. All came together in the redeeming, equalizing act.

[12] In our thinking, myth is not a lie. It is a medium for communicating of truth of the abiding kind that transcends particularity and peculiarly. Truth that is significant regardless of who the current players happen to be.

Chapter Six

The Overcome Unites All Blacks: Christians, Muslims And Rastafarians

The Civil Rights Era, with the agenda it spawned, can be considered the matrix of black philosophy and theology. In this sense, most of black theology becomes interpretation of the new black consciousness as raised during and after the Civil Rights Movement of the 1960's. Because most of the thinking has been rooted in the arena of Christianity, its efficacy for the larger redemption of black people the world over is limited, and we note for the most part that the liberation message is being targeted to the black Christian Church.

But, how would the Muslim blacks get connected in a unifying story if the key reminder of the locale of the essence of religious liberation is only in the Christian Christ? It is through the consideration of notions like these that I gain the courage to say that a man like Martin Luther King, Jr, whose blood has already been shed, and whose elevation could be easily interpreted as the vindication needed before the declaration of the Overcoming/Passover event, is appropriate. An all-inclusive myth could be developed around Dr. King's life, one that offers the uniting, beginning story for the new black hermeneutic.

The "struggle for liberation," conceived in a variety of ways as power—political, educational or economic —devised and controlled from the locale of blacks, is often seen as in opposition to white political and economic power; in opposition to white structures and values. Color is made the key, as blacks are described as somehow "under" and marginal in every way, while whites are perceived to be over and in charge in every way.

Even one generation after the civil rights movements of the 1950's and 1960's; even after the black power movement which grew out of the Civil Rights Movement, and was for a while concurrent with it; even after black theology, which issued from black power and made God and His Jesus black and on the side of the oppressed—who were in the minds of the writers in this field mainly black—even after all these developments, the issue remains the same.

Blacks are still "under" and asking permission even for the acceptance of their self-description. And most arguments place whites in a position, being "over and in authority" and granting or withholding permission to be, to do and become. This is one of the key areas that truly interest me and that must be the focus of any analysis on liberation and the future of blacks in this nation and in the world.

There is a real sense in which the earth-shaking protest demonstrations of Martin Luther King, Jr. were in effect pleadings from a powerless group that needed to carry signs saying "I am a man!" loosely brought together over the perceived need to "struggle" for liberation, justice, equality, and equal opportunity in a land where none of this was real for people of color.

Strange how the "struggle" took the form of a pleading and asking of permission to be and to become. The positive result of all this, however, was the fact that as Dr. King and his followers successfully raised the nation's moral consciousness and sensitivities, with the help of many caring whites I might add, they prepared the way for the instituting of civil rights laws, many of them written and lobbied through Congress by the late Clarence Mitchell, Jr. of the NAACP, known fondly to many as the 101st senator.

In all this, what was offered was a movement, a process, with battles and stages and strategies that could win or fail.

"We must first learn to be reconciled to ourselves lest

we fail to recognize the resources we already have and upon which we can build." (New York Times, 7/31/66) [Statement by the National Committee of Negro Churchmen]

A statement like the above reminds us that we are not totally powerless and need not be forever a race where in 90 percent are beggars seeking sustenance from the oppressor, and at the very minimal levels, or busy envying the 10 percent who are perceived to be making it. The power to overcome is already present and resident in our powerful fraternities, sororities, churches, professional and Greek-lettered organizations. The power is there in our church credit unions and the already established banks and savings and loan organizations.

But, nothing will happen until "group power," much like that developed and exercised in the Jewish communities, becomes the reality of black power and black liberation movements. We do already have many groups. Part of our problem resides in the fact that we have so many groups, each with its different way of "intending to do the redemptive work."

There is no true connectedness, no rooting and grounding. There is no commonly shared genesis and no set of givens accepted by all that can be used to stop the argument. In short, there is no undebatable starting point in the exercise of black liberation thinking.

Everything is up for questioning and for another point of view; and so, there is no specific bugle call that could summon all to the battle front, no way of appealing to a beginning common authority that can force the rallying of all for the next effort needing all the thinking power and the resources available. And so, we continue to do many, many redemptive things, but as individuals and as isolated groups, but nothing that can impact for radical changes.

Black liberation thinking may be bankrupt, stuck as it is in the historical analyses; void of the kind of philosophical/theological springboard that will jump it to the next stage of development where the status of blacks is described differently; and where they are required to behave, live and think out what they already are, by fiat of theological or philosophical description, a liberated people of God who are heirs to all that is God's.

THE OVERCOME

Black clergymen are not without blame and indict themselves from time to time as they "confess the guilt which is ours for past actions and inaction in failing to be instruments for the expression of the will of God as black churchmen."[1] They further acknowledge that "the black church has unwittingly become a tool of oppression, providing an easy vehicle for escape from the harsh realities of our existence. This of necessity makes it impossible for us to be instruments of liberation which is our calling as Christians, and particularly black Christians."[2]

It is not enough to recognize and recall weaknesses and failures, one must go beyond this recall and fix the problem.

The recognition of the problem of the failure in leadership of many black clergy convinces further of the fact that until the leaders in the black community, those who will show the way out for their entrapped people, discover their Overcoming/Passover event; until they, our leaders, learn to sing the song, "We Have Overcome Today," the song of a truly liberated people, all our thinking, talking, preaching, praying and programming will be done in a "hopeful" mood, as we earnestly hope and wait for the day that is yet to be.

There could be no question of our need for a redefinition of ourselves when our leading black theologian, James H. Cone, can say, "Blacks who are struggling to be human in an inhuman world of white racism."[3] The presupposition here is at the heart of what we wish to dispel and reject, the notion that blacks, or any other group for that matter, who are suffering in a peculiar way, are at any stage through the suffering "less than human," and must therefore engage themselves in a struggle, a process, to become human. There is resident here an underlying category mistake, a linguistic trap that conceptually entraps us, making us tame and permitting our leading scholar in the theological interpretation of black pathology to say that "blacks are struggling to be human."

This statement is not at all unlike that seen on some placards during the southern freedom marches with captions saying, "I Am a Man."

If blacks ever accept the presupposition that any acts by others did or could at any time make them less than human, less than men, our redemptive exercise and the approach taken in this work cannot stand. For our first step would not be one of declaring Overcome, but declaring that we are people/human. Since this writer has never had a problem with his humanness—never has that been up for question—we shall continue as though all blacks reading these pages know for sure that they are human, made in the image of God, and that their humanness cannot at any time be taken away or even diminished in its essence.

I truly hope that such could be easily accepted as a "given tenet" that will require no argument. That feeling of "nobodyness" at which Martin Luther King, Jr. points is perhaps at the root of this very claim by Cone that the people for whom he speaks are non-human, struggling to become human.

Such dysfunctional presuppositions in the thinking of black liberationists make our call for a re-definition of who we are something that must happen at the genesis of any black theology of liberation.

The "sociology" of the black situation remains so pathological and overwhelming in the eyes even of the would-be change agents that the beginning description about the given nature of man (for Christians, always sons and daughters of God; His heirs; a little lower than the angels; worthy for Him to dwell with through Incarnation at Christmas; worthy for His son to die for, Good Friday) is completely out of whack.

The mind set of the leading change agents demands a new beginning, a new conceptual starting point that ought to be primarily concerned with the re-definition of black humankind, recognizing that slavery did not and could not make blacks in essence any less than human. Humankind, black or white, needs only to become more and more what it already is in essence.

Thinking that is sociologically-based cannot effectively do this. Our thinkers might need a dose of prescriptive philosophy or dogmatic theology, wherein the ideal is described and made normative.

In other words, what needs to be emphasized and put straight are the forces that limit people from growing into their full stature, not more self-demeaning phrases with the net effect of taking away the very concept about basic humanness required if the arguments for redemption and liberation are to gain force.

Liberation is for humans in bondage, not for non-humans struggling to become human. Part of the conceptual trap this kind of talk established has to do with the fact that it tames the black mind into actually believing that its "status" as human and significant will emerge only after the struggle to be human is successful. In any event, what will count as success criteria in this regard? When does one become human? What features must be present and in what combinations?

What is most needed; what is required before we can move forward is certainly not more black consciousness-raising efforts, a work that has already been done very well by our preachers, theologians and black power advocates.

What is needed is the simple declaration of our Overcoming all these forms of negativity, through an identifiable event in history, resident in a venerable person. What we advocate here will not be seen as black God talk because such talk already has its Passover lamb in the person of Jesus Christ.

What blacks need in terms of an Overcome/Passover event must somehow be grounded at a level sufficiently foundational to include all blacks. It must be able to speak to them, mean for them whether they be Christians (as most are now), Muslims, Jews, Rastafarians, atheists, agnostics or whatever.

Black liberation theology presents and speaks as though all blacks are Christians or even religious. This is not the case.

In some parts of Africa, Muslim is the religion of the majority. In fact, the Overcoming/Passover event for blacks that I here advocate and actually declare in these pages in the name of, and in behalf of blacks the world over, for today, tomorrow and forever, whether they accept it or murmur over my presumption, for a time as did the Israelites of the Exodus, is one done for, and efficacious for all blacks.

When fully understood, and taken into the matrix of our normative conventions, this declaration will represent the first stage of moving from tribalism (denominationally, fraternally, linguistically, complexionally or whateverly based) to a stage of being truly connected at the Genesis/Exodus level.

The call for a Declaration of Independence on the part of blacks is by no means new. The new labelling of the call as the Overcome/Passover event, and the requirement that we locate it in time, in the life of a person who can be uniting, whose life was exemplary and whose life's work has been vindicated and lifted up, these may be new emphases put forward through this work.

But, the need for black independence has already been stated. The first major text of a black Declaration of Independence states, after outlining the litany of the hurts inflicted on blacks by majority America, declares:

> We, therefore, the black people of the United States of America in all parts of this nation, appealing to the Supreme Judge of the world for the rectitude of our intentions, do, in the name of our good people and our own black heroes—Richard Allen, James Varick, Absalom Jones, Nat Turner, Frederick Douglass, Marcus Garvey, Malcolm X, Martin Luther King, Jr. and all black people past, present, great and small, solemnly publish and declare, that we shall be, and of right ought to be, free and independent from the injustice, exploitative control, institutionalized violence and racism of white America, that unless we receive full redress and relief from these inhumanities, we will move to renounce all allegiance to this nation, and will refuse in every way, to cooperate with the Evil which is perpetuated upon ourselves and our communities. And for the support of this declaration, with a firm reliance upon the protection of Divine Providence, we mutually pledge to each other our Lives, our Fortunes, and our sacred Honor.[4]

The above Declaration of Independence contains to some measure some of the basic ingredients necessary for an Overcoming/Passover event. It recognizes our forebears by name, and it recognizes that some things must be solemnly declared and proclaimed. But, its net effect is to state once more some intentions, some hopes and demands.

It solemnly publishes and declares that we "shall be" and "ought to be" free and independent from "injustice, exploitative control, institutionalized violence and racism of white America." But, once again, it is stated in the "shall/ought mood" of the pre-liberation movement.

Though declared, what is being declared is something of an "intention," something that will be in process, and not a "done deal," done at least by God's fiat and action, with the help of the historical heroes listed—forebears, great or small.

More, the declaration of this black independence is not common knowledge among the masses who are to be the beneficiaries of this declared independence. I came across it but recently after having myself come to the conclusion that something like this is needed and the moment through which that can effectively be made to mean is present and not been used efficaciously.

But, this declaration, because it is not known, cannot become part of the public fare. It cannot be forged into the matrix of life-forming conventions from which concepts and values are drawn to be written on the heart, between the eyes and on the door posts. It is not celebrated and thereby remembered with rite and ritual. And that is good. Because as well-intentioned and as much needed as is our Overcoming/Passover event through which we declare our liberation and total independence from our former oppressor, and the form of life and its correlated language that entrapped us for so many years, the above referenced Declaration of Independence is not adequate.

It too is pre-liberation; at the stage of stating intentions and hopes and dreams; at the stage of threatening to do this or that (like the game of boys crossing lines before the fight could get started), it simply cannot be in a "shall or ought mood." It must at some stage of this game be made into a "done deal" that then establishes new tasks for the priests and prophets to sell to the people the appropriate rites and rituals (ceremonies and interpretively compelling language of priest and prophet).

For after the declaration of our Overcoming/Passover event, the nature of the enterprise changes drastically.

A BLACK PASSOVER

Our positions change, our language changes, our dispositions change, our way of looking at the world, our way of intending and doing and relating in the world, all must change from one that is congruent with a people "asking permission for everything" to that of a people who claim their resources and make them function for their collective survival.

And, no longer will theologians codify events as part of any "struggle to be human," but such will be forced to write about the transformation, first in attitude, character and positioning, all in the enterprise of making manifest, what already is, our liberation through the life, ministry, death and elevated vindication of the chosen one. The examples for substantiating such thinking exists in the Bible, in the typology of Messiahs and suffering servants.

I am firmly convinced that this "given-like" beginning declaration of our Overcoming/Passover event must somehow become the real starting point for any black theology of liberation. If we are to speak to our black brothers and sisters from the "Overcome mood" rather from the same identical boat of together hoping with them (don't we need a saved person in order to save the unsaved?), our identification and declaration of this Overcoming/Passover event cannot be in any sense tenuous, tentative halting or itself disunifying. It must be at core simple, easy to understand and accept as an authoritative given, a universally accepted tenet, with a well-developed ceremony, complete with ritualistic rites, through which the moment is caught, recalled and celebrated each year; and from which fundamental creedal statements about our re-described selves, our individual and corporate responsibilities within the new community that sees differently, are transmitted to our children, reinforced in our adults, and installed into the corpus of conventions that will in turn help to frame our conceptualizing about ourselves and the language we use to define ourselves and our place in the world.

It is recognized that this is the age for questioning all things, all motives, etc., but we must realize that like the Jews who never bring critical questions to the Passover event of Egypt, and like Christians who find a way to skirt over critical issues regarding their Passover event located in the Good Friday/Easter message, so too, we need to dare to develop that uniting story about how we Overcame/passed over, knowing exactly what we are doing and why; using facts of history and the language of myth as effectively as possible to wrought once and for all time the redemptive act. This is an act that will establish the page break, the before/after interpretive framework for black salvation history.

In the before times, it was permissible to sing, "We Shall Overcome Someday," but in the after period, our new song is about an achievement, a done deal that needs not be done ever again. The new song is, "We Have Overcome Today."

Black power expresses most keenly what needs to be done after the Overcome/Passover event. For it offers an essentially black value system, with its life-saving set of rules. It attempts to fine tune black culture to include the givenness of the Passover so that it could be expressed in its poetry, songs, religious services and in the general language and parlance of the populace.

I dare say that black power as a notion failed precisely because its call for power to the people preceded the identification of the Overcoming/Passover event. And so, an underpeople, a powerless people, powerless by self-description (not in reality) seeks power and gains only more good rhetoric. Preliminary to developing and managing power, therefore, must be the Overcoming/Passover event, followed by a process of building life-saving institutions.

After our Overcoming/Passover event has been identified, accepted, celebrated and itself institutionalized, all actions that will require some major iconoclastic moves on the part of blacks, who to a larger degree than many have dared to express, remain in the pre-liberation state because our true problems are not external or imposed, but internal and conceptual at the core.

They have much to do with our conceptual imaging, and so part of the criteria for determining the success at this stage of the game would be discovering whether blacks can effectively "break" some of the pre-liberation images, thereby becoming iconoclastic.

The need for becoming truly iconoclastic, by breaking the pre-liberation value images, particularly those in the churches, cannot be emphasized enough. It will require,

A BLACK PASSOVER

as an act of the Overcoming/Passover event, actions that will result in our physically removing (taking them down) and making presents of them to our white Christian brothers the white images that dominate our black churches.

If our white Christian brothers will not receive them, then we should destroy them. Remember, how Moses, on returning from the mountaintop reacted to the "false" images of the newly liberated people.

Moses was one of the first iconoclasts, prepared to break any image that would prove dysfunctional to his task of nation-building. So, we will need, an appropriate ceremony, to take down the images of the oppressors and return them, sell them or burn them.

This is not unlike what newly independent countries do on Independence Day. At a specific time, in the presence of the colonizer and with due ceremony, after the playing of the oppressor's national anthem, its flag is slowly lowered while at the same time the flag of the newly independent nation is slowly raised.

Never mind the fighting, the negotiating, the planning and designing of a constitution and new flag that went on before, independent status is achieved only after a lowering of the key symbol of what was being displaced and the raising of the key symbol of what the future will be. The national anthem of the pre-liberation stage is like "We Shall Over Someday," and the national anthem of the Overcome people is like "We Have Overcome Today."

In areas of Cone's work, he precisely states the nature of the new way of thinking that must be put in place. "Jesus' Resurrection is the good news that there is new life for the poor that is not determined by their poverty, but overcomes it, and this new life is available to all."[5] He continues to further explain his point by showing that, "If this Biblical message has any meaning for contemporary America, it must mean that black power represents God's resurrection in Jesus becoming embodied in the consciousness and actions of black America."[6]

At least the foretaste of a black Overcoming/Passover event is here resident (overcoming through participating in the resurrection event), but lacking of the "achievement," mastery, once-for-all-time-ness of the issue.

The major thrust of black liberation has been in reaction to white racism, and a revolution of sorts was developed to shake the foundations. And yet, years after, all we have is more rhetoric and more books. But, we need neither the revolution nor the reaction.

The simple declaration of our Overcome, followed by the development of the appropriate covenant relationships with basic rules of life and a method for claiming the ghetto—or whatever land we can get—as we go about the business of building every life-saving institution in our various communities—for the welfare and well-being of our redeemed people of the Overcome era—is all we need. The rest has already being put in place by the many trailblazers who went before us. They set the stage.

For the fight is not only against racism, capitalism and imperialism as we love to pretend, all forces external to us. But, it is also against our tendency to self-destruct and our failure to trust our brothers and our institutions (hospitals, banks, builders and not totally without cause).

Recently, in Baltimore, Provident Hospital went out of business for lack of patients. Weeks later, under a new name, but in the same location with many of the same black nurses and doctors, the hospital is fully occupied and profitable.

Blacks, during our watch over this institution, successfully killed what our forebears had built over a 90-year period. One could hear blacks actually saying, "Don't take me to Provident." Even a nurse who was working there was heard by me, while on a pastoral visit to the hospital, say with a laugh, "If I am sick, take me to Sinai Hospital."

So all our problems are not external to us. Many are of our own making. Some of our problems are located in the names we call each other, so gross and demeaning, they cannot be printed. Even the adjectives to use to describe our brothers' mothers, our partners and buddies is downing. A key descriptive creed in our black communities is a saying: "Niggers ain't —it." The latter is indeed more than a statement and truly encapsules the most prevalent self-description one can find in many black communities.

Of course, many readers might want to deny this

A BLACK PASSOVER

statement. Should they, then they will be doing no more than attempting to build on a lie. The fact remains that in these and other ways, too crude to mention, the evidence abounds that blacks are the hardest on themselves in term of self-description. And they seem to have examples for their descriptions. Have you heard the one that describes blacks as "crabs in a basket"? In this, the belief is held that one black will not help the other out of poverty (I'm not going to make the n——r rich) and would do whatever it takes to sabotage the other's progress.

Again, you are mad with me.

But in this case my evidence is first-hand. My wife once owned two neighborhood grocery stores, and the "crab syndrome" came alive in and through these.

First, the black neighbors did all they could to prevent the transfer of the necessary license to operate one store, using every legal maneuver. But, when a couple years later, my wife got ready to sell the store to Koreans, despite the fact the city wrote letters to the leaders of the community, being sure they would continue their protest; despite the fact that they delayed the hearing, certain that the community would make every attempt to stop the transfer of the license, not one community resident appeared to protest the license transfer to the Koreans.

But, two busloads were raised in order to protest the transfer of the license to fellow blacks. More, the stores were broken into almost nightly, vandalized as the intruders trampled on goods they could not take, and in the act that really drove my wife out of business, when they broke in one Saturday night, after taking all they could, after trampling on the rest, they took time to defecate, yes, leave human feces on the floor of a store that had a bathroom.

What a statement! My wife sold out to a Korean who has not had one problem. Lesson. I am myself totally convinced that blacks who do this are in effect trying to protect the lie about why so many are black, poor and in trouble.

It is logically required that they stop anyone of their number who attempts to rise and succeed, despite the same experiences from the same negative environment. If the other succeeds, being black and from the same situation, he gives a lie to the explanation.

THE OVERCOME

And so, without even critically analyzing the why of the "crab in the basket" syndrome, he attacks to protect his explanation of his plight.

This is another of the reasons why I am certain that we need a black Overcome/Passover event, which would be used as catalyst to start the process of self-description as a people.

For without a radical break with the past, contrived through the establishment of the Overcome, before/after break, the new teaching cannot be grounded. There will always be that sense that we tried that already, and it did not help. There is so much of that "we have tried that already" feeling.

Why? Because the Overcome/Passover event has not yet brought an end to the old way of seeing and doing, clearing the way for teaching the new way. And, blacks are like rafters in the torrents of the rapids; like people caught in a whirlpool with a bottomless pit under it.

Should we never find the conceptual means through which we stop, make and take the Overcoming break, so that we could start again, we shall surely remain frustrated and tired as if in the rapids or whirlpool with dangers everywhere, disorder and chaos as the norm and imminent danger as the most likely outcome.

I continue to believe that the old way of seeing and talking must come to an end, a dated end. The new way of seeing, talking and doing must begin. This must happen around some significant historical event or experience of black people and must serve as the marker. For anyone with the ability to reflect will realize that just as World War I and World War II had to end before Europe or Japan could start rebuilding, so too must the struggle and fight, as viewed by blacks, come to a declared end, so that the building age and stage could be instituted.

It is conceptually impossible (or at least foolish) to start rebuilding at a time when one is sure that the enemy will just come and break it down before it is finished. Could you imagine Coventry Cathedral being re-built during the bombing raids on England? Must not all the efforts go into the war?

It is only after the battle that the rebuilding can seriously begin—unless we take another example from Jewish scripture where the Jews re-built while keeping

A BLACK PASSOVER

their swords with them. Something must come to an end; the old way of seeing must die. And, from this death must spring a new way of seeing, talking, being and doing in the world.

That is why we need, not more rhetoric, theology or philosophy, but a simple story, a coherent larger than life myth that can be made to speak to blacks simply and individually, but also to all corporately. In a real sense, only the language of myth can do this, and it is most unfortunate that we must start building our mythology after Bultmann has called for demytholization and in the contemporary world in which most people believe that a myth is a lie. How sad!

The story about George Washington, father of this nation, who never told a lie, what is that if not a recent myth? But, what a message to the youth about telling the truth with the possibility of becoming the president. We do need this myth, re-describing ourselves and the process of the victory through whomever we choose, so that we can move forward and develop new descriptions of who we are and how we may define ourselves and our brothers.

We are currently the chieftains at stopping ourselves from real progress. We already control in excess of $204 billion, and we will not make this work for us. We will not make our neighbors rich by supporting in a deliberate way their business and making them accountable. Not realizing that in helping the neighbor to success, we can be helping ourselves and our posterity. Make the brother rich and have your son to marry his daughter.

Multiply that several times and so create some aspects of the Vision Glorious. But, we don't do that. Blacks are willing to follow a Jim Jones, trust him to the jungles of Guyana and unto death, but not the black brother. For Jones was perhaps the first white man showing care, showing that blacks and whites could indeed walk hand in hand.

And this being the dream of so many blacks, not to build themselves, but to be accepted and integrated, that they come to integration not as equals, not as a people who have overcome. They come to such relationships as the "under class" seeking authentication.

Even some of our black leaders, and sporting stars,

THE OVERCOME

even some Black Panthers married whites, before they declared their Overcome, in many cases seeking status. In modern days, many of our black celebrities are wearing contact lens to make their eyes blue or green. And this, before their Overcoming/Passover event.

In all our liberation thinking, talking and doing, one key question has not been raised or answered. I dare to raise it now. For, apart from a generally accepted understanding of the answer to this very question, we will never know when our initial work has been accomplished. The question: "What can serve as success criteria within the black liberation effort?"

Is there any true, consistent picture of what is being sought, so that when "it" has arrived we could all know? Dr. King sought his "Beloved Community" perhaps with the "walking hand in hand imagery." Is such the picture of that which will count for success? Is that truly our Vision Glorious? Others seek "Black Power," but what is that and how does one know when one has it? And how much of either picture must be in the bag before we can say, "We've got it"?

Part of the reason for the failure of black liberation thinking to bring about black liberation is the fact that it is given, for the most part, to the chronicling of pathology, and hence remains mostly devoid of any major successes. One who is looking at the situation would wonder whether there is nothing there to "give thanks for," nothing yet accomplished, nothing yet completed.

I wonder whether these black liberation writers can truly say "thanks" for anything accomplished. Can they say, "Thanks Martin for that which you accomplished in and on our behalf"? It is as though blacks generally believe that it is indeed dangerous to say thanks, to claim any "Overcoming" or done deals, because such would set the stage for complacency, resting on our laurels while little gains are taken back from us.

But, it is precisely in this area that we must look for the key to real liberation. And, we might need to claim some major once-for-all-time victory in and through Martin Luther King, so that we can chalk-up at least one done deal, done for our people and by our people, an event through which we gained symbolic parity with all other peoples of this nation. And, recognizing that there is much work ahead to be accomplished, much catching up and surpassing to do, go about the business of celebrating what we have already achieved while gearing up for what we yet have to do.

Chapter Six Notes

[1] Wilmore/Cone. Black Theology. "The Church and Urban Crisis," p. 44.

[2] Ibid., p. 46.

[3] James Cone. "For My People," p. 20.

[4] "Black Declaration of Independence" cited in Wilmore/Cone. Black Theology, pp. 110 ff.

[5] Cone. "For My People," p. 33.

[6] Ibid., p. 33.

Chapter Seven

Concept Analysis: Key to Black Liberation Thinking

Liberation talk, like all other talk, is riddled with conceptual puzzlements, many of them resulting from the unexamined use of liberation language. Here I offer a method for fitting each piece of the conceptual puzzle into its rightful place.

Using the method of Ludwig Wittgenstein and Gilbert Ryle, I attempt to offer pointers to ways of clarifying perplexities in our thinking and talking in this area by producing a possible interpretive grammar for the new disciplines of black liberation theology and philosophy.

If the problems in the disciplines can be likened to being trapped, like a fly in a bottle, by our situation and the concepts we use to handle that situation, then our true task becomes one of showing the way out conceptually. This is a preliminary move to freedom from entrapment within the given form of life. In the varying fields of ethics, theology, logic and even jurisprudence, thinkers have turned to the linguistic philosopher for pointers on how conceptual analysis can clear up perplexities within the field. It is suggested here that black liberation thought can truly benefit from this method also.

Of course, it is only a method. There are no tenets or doctrines at this level—nothing to be adopted. We shall, however, boldly move from this purely descriptive

THE OVERCOME

approach to the prescriptive, and through this move demonstrate that a part of the grammar of liberation requires a prescribing of a new order, a new status and new success criteria, which will tell us when we have mastered the issue, problem or situation at hand.

By using the method of concept analysis, many of the key epistemological, pedagogical, and psychological concepts used can be analyzed and laid bare so that we can see whether they are of the fabric of dispositions, abilities, skills or activities. One can easily become confused by seeing a concept such as "understanding" as an *activity* word, pointing to an activity of the mind, which could be identified, measured, clocked, rather than as a *dispositional/mastery* word, pointing to a capacity to be and do in certain ways.

I believe that part of the conceptual entrapment experienced by black liberation thinkers is located here. There is a tendency to mix categories, making the category mistakes that lock us in and tame us as a people. When one listens even to the brightest, most articulate, even wealthy black, one can sense a certain language entrapment. Though his form of life, his total sophistication, says and demonstrates that he has "overcome," his language cannot say it. Why? The language, set as it is in the "shall mood," the "someday mode" prevents him from declaring what he is. His success, measured by any standard, any form of life, would authenticate his language of success, but for some reason, it cannot be stated.

One intent of this book is to force upon us all the notion that we must at some point know and state what counts for success in this struggle, or we will struggle forever. Nineteen eighty-nine will have the exact same concerns as 2089, if the page break, the Passover is not established at some point.

And this will not work because at some point we must account for the success of Oprah Winfrey, Eddie Murphy, Reginald Lewis, Bill Cosby and a host of other successful blacks who have in every sense of the word overcome the negative stoppers. If these people are not to be considered special, then the language must shift. Then it would admit that all have not yet succeeded at the same level (but all whites are not rich or happy or oppressing, either, and many, no doubt envy Michael Jackson, Bruce Llewelyn and Congressman William Gray).

The argument soon helps us to realize that "success words," mastery words through which we declare we now "have it" so we can continue the series on our own as we go on to do a multitude of things from our new operating stance, are precisely what are most lacking on the tongue of blacks, their thinkers, teachers and above all, their preachers. When Paul Holmer implies that black religion, the chief change agent in the black community, is about singing dirges (death songs), and that black theology is then seen as the descant upon the dirge—with no real victorious thing to hang the black corporate hat on—we quickly see the extent of our entrapment.

Part of the puzzlement you will recognize resides in the closeness of some of the concepts used in liberation thinking. It is not unlike the relatedness of some of the concepts used in education: reading, thinking, remembering, calculating, knowing, understanding. They are all related, but another look shows that they are different "types" or categories of words. Understanding, for example, requires some aspects of teaching, reading, thinking, calculating and even remembering.

But, reading, thinking, and calculating are obviously activities of the mind. They each have a beginning and an ending; they could be stopped and started again. Time span is always involved. Understanding, on the other hand, is not an activity. Can one understand for one hour and then stop? Understanding is rather a dispositional or capacity word and never just one more mental activity, like reading or calculating.

In a very real sense, understanding is, to coin a phrase, a first-order concept. Once one arrives at understanding, one is freed to form, shape and govern one's own life in that area instead of being forever passively framed, shaped and governed from without by the environment or whatever. People who have achieved understanding, a capacity, can actively form their own lives.

In like manner, liberation as a concept is of the nature or type we call dispositional or mastery concepts. It is an achievement, mastery or status word, a "first-order concept" that tells whether one has taken control of one's future to the point at which one is freed indeed to form, shape and govern one's own life, with the capacity and power to rearrange all the given furniture of life in such a way as to enhance and sustain the newly-achieved liberation status.

Black liberation thinkers have tended to seek methods and principles from other philosophies and theologies, like Marxism and theology of hope. They seek their cues from these disciplines. Marxism, as a method of social analysis, is particularly attractive to these thinkers. They start with the method (the grammar) of Marxism, but soon they are quietly adopting the tenets, integrated as they are in the method of Marxism.

There is an inherent problem in this tendency to seek authenticity from any "ism." For often a kind of conceptual enslavement results as they take sides and fine tune tenets and creeds. What we are attempting to do is dependent on the acceptance of the fact that the foundation of any liberation theology or philosophy cannot be based on an "ism," a party issue.

The most fundamental questions are never those that can be captured in an "ism." At this level, we need foundational, "transismatic" approaches, which do not set the stage for any affiliation to the tenets of any party. For it remains true that all "isms" are philosophically questionable. They get their name as an "ism" by being opposed by the newest rival "ism." And to build any liberation foundation on an "ism" is to build on a disputable foundation.[1]

Liberation thinking that patterns itself after traditional philosophy will fall into the trap of seeking out the referents of certain key concepts. Such a procedure assumes that the true nature of concepts is found in their referents. Hence, in order to become clear on a concept like justice or liberty, the philosopher had to show whether the concept was referenced in nature, was supra-mundane, a psychological existent or simply a private intuition. We watched as they sought "the meaning" of this or that concept and as the intelligentsia demanded that we "define your terms."

We are off on the wrong track when we believe that the key issue being discussed is simply about words and their meanings. For one thing, words have no meaning in and of themselves, but find meaning on the lips and in the lives of competent persons with the permission to use them.

A BLACK PASSOVER

And a little reflection will remind us that the person who learns a language has the capacity and the permission to use the words and concepts of that language in all the stock and non-stock language games permissible. For, one in learning the language is not first taught the meanings of words, but is taught how to use words like "if," "head," "ought, "this" and "that." And if it were otherwise, what would count as the meaning of "if" or "when"?

The pointing out of this simple fact becomes important when we make our strategic appeal to the change agents within the black community to deliberately search out some of the key missing concepts and realize that they will never, indeed, can never, become real apart from our developing the process whereby they are learned and installed so that they can in turn become part of that which will fashion new lives, liberated and successful lives.

Remember that if one truly understands the meaning of a word or concept, one with that also understands all its possible uses. And this simply prepares one (poises him with a certain capability) to do a lot of things with the word or concept. Every schoolboy knows that quite often the meaning of a word does not depend upon the sentences in which it fits, but sometimes on the paragraph, the work, the age of the book.

Consequently, on recognizing the setting, the linguistic game type that is here applicable: fiction, Holy Scripture, creeds, joking, poetry, the reporting of facts or the recounting of a dream, one can normally, and with a certain degree of ease, figure (a type of calculating) what is up. To push this argument one step further, one might say that some of the meanings that words might have depend on the person's stage of development. That might be one reason for our being so tolerant with the language of children and madmen, and so intolerant with mistakes made by the college student, or university professor who mishandles language. Again, a matter of competence and not just about words anymore.

No attempt will be made here to offer any new knowledge. The author is not seeking to offer another opinion, another truth or develop new truths about reality. If one were to inquire as to my motive, I would need to declare that I perceive blacks in America and the world to be trapped in a conceptual prison and are desperate to find a way out. They have tried just about everything so far, except conceptual analysis.

I happen to believe that the problem of black liberation is conceptual, psychological, cultural, economic and political. And, I further believe that the way to understanding the conceptual entrapment black thinkers and writers find themselves is via the route of conceptual analysis.

The father of conceptual analysis, Ludwig Wittgenstein, once said of his philosophical task, "What is philosophy: to show the fly the way out of the fly bottle."[2] The fly is entrapped and confused over finding a passage to the exit. The real philosopher would come to the aid of the fly and simply show the way out. Now, the showing of the fly the way out does not entail of necessity any great philosophical treatise on the nature of the captivity, specific, or captivity in general. It needs no analysis of the virtues of freedom or about the texture of the bottle prison. All that is needed is the pointing of the way out.

This should be the task of the black liberation thinker who perceives that his people are trapped in an ongoing, undesirable state of oppression and should be released. Black thinkers no doubt recognize this. However, to date, they have tended to further describe the pathology, themselves often appearing trapped by the same situation, and consequently, they have not succeeded in showing the way out of the bondage. And how could they when they are using methods not appropriate for dealing with the conceptual problem that is at the heart of the liberation issue?

The strange fact remains that the way to solve the problem and show the way out of the perplexity that can be adequately described as "poor, black and in real trouble" is the fact that nothing needs to be manufactured. All we need is already there in the language and the body of conventions that inform us—in our Bible stories, in our religions.

What we must do now is clear up the messy, slovenly use of language by revealing even to the man on the street just how the "deeper" controlling grammar of our common language can be used to show blacks that "the strife is over, the battle done," and that they have already over-

A BLACK PASSOVER

come the very obstacles that they believe are still in their way.

By looking at language in a new way, we will soon discover that the interpretive grammar of our language has a way of covering and accounting for "isness" and "oughtness." And it is in the contemplation of these very issues that we get to the heart of the black liberation problem. What "is" and what "ought to be," and how it comes to be. One could hardly raise any question that is fundamentally more philosophic or conceptual for that matter. Our leading linguistic philosophers will show that such are indeed conceptual issues and in the interpretive grammar of the language one can find all the extant rules that govern, and the descriptions that cover not only the indicative and imperative aspects of the concepts in a language, but also the conditional, fictitious, scientific, factual, poetic, etc.

Many people continue to believe that words are like names with real referents there in the world. But, it shall be demonstrated that many of the psychological words, like liberation, do not in fact name anything, but simply serve as human descriptions of dispositions, behavior tendencies or status. Conflicts can occur because very often people who are pursuing very different interests wrongly assume that because another uses the same words, the criteria for judging the results will be the same. This does nothing more than set the stage for people to continue to talk past each other without hearing.

In what I am attempting to do, there is no intention of offering new knowledge or new facts. The facts are already there and the analyses of them are adequate. But, I wish to remind the reader that sometimes what is most needed is not to discover or see something new, but rather the discovering of a "new way of seeing" what is already there, but in a new light; with a different set of spectacles and from a different mood and stance.

We shall seek only to show the fly the way out of the fly bottle. We seek only to make the known facts more clear by offering an interpretive framework for the viewing, arranging and taking of the same old facts of the matter, a new way of looking at the facts, never pretending to have discovered any new facts. So we look at the language, seeing our task as one of revealing likenesses and differences, truths, untruths and half-truths that may be concealed in the language in such a way as to connote falsely and dysfunctionally.

In short, through the method of concept analysis, we seek not to reconstruct reality, but rather to point out tenable theories, clarify conceptual confusions, linguistic stoppers, and try on the whole to avert the mishandling of the key concepts used in liberation thinking, as it applies to blacks in this instance.

Follow our arguments, and you will soon discover that certain utterances can be authentic apart from being true or false in the classic sense. And by the same token, utterances can be "infelicitous" in many other ways than being just untrue. There is only one way to do this and it is via what is called concept analysis.

Concept Analysis

Concept analysis is nothing more than a method, for there are no tenets or positions to put forth. And yet, it is difficult to underwrite the method of concept analysis. One must, as it were, look and see how the professionals go about doing concept analysis and achieve the goal of clearing up key confusions that can prevent us from grasping the significance of certain concepts. For the method is concealed in speaking grammatically. Despite the difficulty in describing the method, however, we will use an example to demonstrate how it is best done.

Gilbert Ryle, a master at doing this, offers the example via certain discussions about "mind." He begins by reminding us that the popular view of mind can best be characterized as a "ghost in a machine,"[3] mind being considered the name of that immaterial, occult substance peculiar to humans. Then through the use of paradigm cases of the word mind at work in a language, he shows that mind is not a naming, naming any one thing, but rather a concept.

Classically, mind names the innerman, and is seen as a noun with a referent, although admittedly an invisible referent. Ryle shows that mind as a concept names no one thing, but is used with a variety of nuances in a rich variety of ways, and often in conjunction with many subconcepts that are closely related one to another.

Within the range of nuances contained in the word

A BLACK PASSOVER

mind are some activities like calculating, reading, remembering and thinking. There are also some dispositions like caring, intending, believing, understanding and wanting. And there are capacities and abilities such as those which point to our being able to do and to behave in such and such ways. Through concept analysis, one can become clear as to whether *mind*, or aspects of mind as used in a given context, point to an *ability, activity, capacity* or *disposition*.

It was my study in this very area that led me to believe that the essence of liberation thinking must be arrived at via a similar method. We shall soon discover why it was necessary to follow this detour, one that initially seems to have no bearing on the matter under discussion. But it does.

Ludwig Wittgenstein did concept analysis around psychological words like: fearing, wishing, understanding, intending, thinking, willing and knowing. He also showed that many of our key psychological words are used to point to activities, skills, dispositions, tendencies, propensities and capacities of humans.

Ryle offers another example in his discussion of the word "know." He shows that within the concept of knowing there is a certain "knowing that" and a "knowing how to." There are certain parallels and diversions between "knowing that" and "knowing how to." This should be obvious to all. But often, if little points are not made, people tend to pass them over and make key category mistakes that could prove dysfunctional to understanding the issues at hand.

Black liberation thinkers have not yet looked to conceptual analysis for the breakdown of the flag word, liberation. They have not even done it in terms of the word black. And so, in classic style, we find them trying desperately to connect with some tried and tested philosophy or theology.

Some try to connect with Marxism, seeking the method for analysis there; others look to the theology of hope, process theology and other forms of liberation theology. Each takes a position; in each case, the tenets of the operative theology or philosophy are adopted and the process of adaptation to fit the black situation begins. As a consequence, we witness the rise of new brands of black liberation theology, each with its tenets.

Dr. King has his Vision Glorious (beloved community) that contradicts Malcolm X's vision of the nation within a nation, or Marcus Garvey's migrationism. Even within the very young field of black theology, this has begun to occur. The process of taking sides and stating positions has begun. And some will become enslaved to their particular "ism." For us, however, there can be no room for "isms" at the basic level of liberation philosophy. For the issues important in party ("ism") philosophy are not fundamental when each depends on the incorrectness of the other.[4]

At the most basic level, division cannot be made part of the foundational logic in the redemptive process. Black liberation theology is at that critical junction where it has begun to develop its party issues, setting the stage from which young thinkers simply develop the technique of assuming a religious discipleship to the tenets of the perceived authorities, and do thinking as though it were a process of acquiring tenets and articles of belief and sharing them with others.

As is the case in philosophy, all "isms" and all party issues are questionable. They gain their very names as "isms" after being attacked and opposed by other "isms" and party issues. And, to develop a liberation theology around a party issue like Marxism or migrationism is to start off by forming a foundation on a disputable position. This could be a sign of mental frailty or downright parasitism.

Consequently, we shall not attempt to develop any new theory, rather we shall seek to clarify some of the fundamental misunderstandings and the resulting confusion in the language of black liberation. There will be no romantic adherence to the thoughts of any of the liberation thinkers, but I shall offer some remarks that could in turn, I hope, serve as starting points for the reader's own investigation.

As suggested above, no new data will be offered; no new theory to oppose anything that is already there will be offered. All we can offer at this time is new and different ways of looking at the facts we already have at hand, forcing us to notice precisely that which has gone unnoticed because it is so familiar and so simple.

I dare to say that black liberation talk, like all other

A BLACK PASSOVER

talk, is riddled with its share of conceptual puzzlements. These often cause, in the words of Wittgenstein, mental cramps and knots in our thinking. Our pre-defined task is one of fitting the pieces of the conceptual puzzlement into their proper linguistic and conventional place. I hope through this process to offer an interpretive grammar for this new field of black liberation theology, simply by looking at the language, the form of life that informs and governs that language and the body of conventions by which the entire enterprise is authenticated.

To jump some stages ahead of ourselves, I might here declare that in cases where certain key concepts are absent from the language, the form of life and the body of conventions, I will dare to show why such concepts are needed, how they get developed and placed so that in turn they inform and govern lives. One such concept, to further jump the gun and offer some inclination of just where this argument is going, is "success criteria," or forms of triumphalism, concepts which appear to be absent from the operative language of the black liberation thinkers.

The idea of using concept analysis to deal with some of the conceptual puzzlements in the thinking of black liberation scholars is not radical. The method has already been successfully used in the various fields of ethics, theology, jurisprudence, political science and logic and is successfully clearing up perplexities in those fields of endeavor.

I think that liberation thinking can benefit from this also.

Of course, all that is really offered is the method. There are really no doctrines or tenets to be adopted. (Except in the few cases where I will dare to demonstrate the need for the introduction of certain notions and concepts that are key to the true understanding and institution of liberation, concepts that have not yet been installed in the language and life of those who are yet in the pre-liberation stage of life.)

Even here, these will not be new concepts, but concepts which are part of the common and shared language which we simply refuse to make work in our lives.

By using this method of concept analysis, the major "mind" concepts used by black liberation thinkers are analyzed to show whether they are of the fabric of dispositions, abilities, skills or activities. One can become very confused and paralyzed from seeing a concept such as liberation as an activity word, pointing to activities of the mind which could be identified, clocked, and measured, rather than as a status or dispositional word. Activities are always measurable. And the nature of liberation is somewhat different, as I shall show.

Conceptual analysis is ideally fitted for examining certain key psychological concepts.

For example, a major aim in liberation talk has to do with truly "understanding" what is being said. The techniques or means to "understanding" are other word/concepts like reading, thinking, remembering, calculating, recalling, etc. But most of these very words point to concepts which are different in texture from understanding itself. Reading, calculating, even thinking are all activities. The paradigm for an activity is anything that has a beginning and an ending, that which could be clocked, stopped and started again.

Time span is always involved. But understanding is not itself an activity. One cannot understand for one hour and then not. Rather, understanding is a concept that points to a disposition, capacity, or achieved status. It is not one more mental activity like thinking, calculating or reading. In a real sense, understanding is a first-order concept. Once one arrives at understanding, once one gains it, one is freed to form, shape and govern one's life, instead of being forever passively framed, shaped and governed from without by the environment, or time, whatever.

It will be a short step, at the right moment, to move from the analysis of understanding, to that of liberation, and joyfully discover that liberation is of the same texture as the word/concept understanding. People who have attained or mastered or grasped understanding (liberation) a capacity can actively form their own lives and the lives of others.

Acquiring Concepts

Concepts are learned when one learns a language. Consequently, one learns the concept of understanding or overcoming or liberty by learning, often by osmosis, the rich variety of language games (linguistic contexts) in which those words can be properly used.

Hence we learn to say "I understand and he understands" or "He does not understand" after we have mastered the various stock and non-stock uses of the word. It will in time become evident that understand just like Overcome/Passover is made up of a much larger family of concepts. And those, too, are mastered in time as one develops competency in the language.

Part of the black liberation problem resides in the fact that some key concepts like "Overcome" have not yet been installed in the informing body of conventions as anything but a "yet to be achieved" notion. And as a result, the thinking and talking, all of it—even the singing about Overcoming/Passover—is done in a future mood (shall), but never as a done deal.

I will show in time that concepts are not only learned and mastered, but that they in turn, after one truly learns and masters them, themselves become the masters, informing and limiting the horizons of him who first learned them.

There is no question that we learn the concepts—red, pain, hot, overcome, liberty—when we learn the language. As indicated above, we do this when we learn the stock/standard ways of using the concepts together with the non-stock or extended ways of talking with the same words. And yet, in the minds of most readers, if asked to define or analyze a word like understanding or liberty, one might go looking for some strange phenomena in the world. But, while phenomena are important, discovering how these concepts actually function in our lives, by forming and governing them, is also very important work.

Anyone can look at phenomena and arrive at some adequate description of them. This is not true in the case of concept analysis. Skills are required here. For it requires the digging up of all the possible uses of concepts in their stock and non-stock contexts and discovering whether as used such concepts can serve well or otherwise. For, quite often in analysis, concepts soon get linked up with human powers: propensities, capacities dispositions and activities and are no longer viewed as words alone. Concepts like liberation do more to signify certain human powers, capacities and status of character than anything else.

And at some point, the assignment must be given requiring that black people who feel oppressed and under, go about the business of nurturing these capacities and powers signified by the concepts of the language.

One may note the ease with which the switch is made from words and concepts to human powers and capacities. This movement from and to words and concepts and human capabilities, tendencies, propensities and powers is a rather significant one. In more senses than one, it can prove to be the most important message to be gained from the examination of the true nature of the concepts.

We generally think that in all cases in which a concept is used in a language that there is some definition or interpretation of the word that can permit it to mean something. We continue for the most part to believe this, forgetting that inability to grasp meaning is something like color blindness. The color blind person is in a real sense lacking or missing a certain ability, capacity or competency necessary for discrimination between colors and shades.

Whenever a capacity is lacking, one is unable to do the things made possible by having that capacity. That is why the color blind person is "unable" to distinguish between colors and shades. Such incapacitation, that is having no powers in a given area of thinking or endeavor, severely limits the range of a person's capabilities. And having that capacity "enables or empowers" one to think and talk and do in ways not possible if the capacity were lacking.

The consequence of this type of argument is that it forces on us the understanding that the teaching and acquiring of new concepts, concepts like Overcoming are not tantamount to the teaching or acquiring of just one more piece of language. Rather, the teaching of conceptual abilities (to go on and effect, bring to pass) is bound up in the actual teaching of the concept. For concepts, like tastes and moral truths, once learned, shape and form outlooks, drives, desires and hopes.

Hence, when one develops the taste for wine, one assumes a new character and power (not redemptively significant) that empowers one to judge and discriminate between wines. In like manner, when one grasps a concept like liberty or honesty, one has not just learned another word, but one also knows what counts as honesty and liberty and what does not. One also desires to be honest or liberated, and feels shame or distress in being otherwise. And concepts like liberation, when truly grasped and fully understood, carry with them something of a moral imperative to be and do the liberating (or honest) thing.

It should be obvious that concepts are more than meet the eye. For they often mix, in a strange way, their imperative and indicative forms. To clarify this strange claim on which some of the arguments in this book will be based, consider the fact that the act of telling someone about something as innocent as a description of icy roads in an apparently disinterested fashion carries with it an "un-said" or non-linguistic imperative to the would-be traveller to be careful on those icy roads.

This is the case. One who truly understands the concepts used to describe icy roads cannot then go on to disregard the hidden unspoken imperative. Such must be careful.

The same happens to be true in black liberation talk. The pathological descriptions, the desperation that goes with the task, carries a hidden imperative that must be heeded. I think that the only reason why it has not been effectively addressed so far is the fact that aspects of the concepts true to liberation, though present in the common language we share with the oppressor, have not been incorporated and installed in the key conventions that inform the guidance system that will effect the changes that are necessary.

And a major part of this work will have to do with the demonstration of the need to install this aspect of the concept into the operational language of blacks in general and their liberation thinkers in particular. This is so that the Overcome "I can do and effect" aspects of the liberating, psychological and epistemological concepts can be indeed grafted into the language, the form of life and also the developing body of conventions that inform and govern our lives.

It should by now be fully apparent that concepts are more than words. Black liberation thinkers, and all change agents, be they preachers or teachers, should know this fact. For concepts have powers over how people's lives are formed, since the learning of concepts fashions how judgments, tastes, desires, drives, intentions are developed, formed and get applied.

Concept Analysis
And Some Key Psychological Concepts

Names and concepts such as dog, table and car are never as problematic as certain psychological, educational (nurturing) and epistemological concepts such as "teach," "learn," "understand," "know," and liberty.Although names like dog and car are themselves not without the possibility of confusing usage, at base they are not problematic words. Perhaps this is because, for the most part, they very often do have identifiable referents that can serve readily as criteria for their authentic usages.

Should one say, "There goes a man"; another can observe-investigate and agree or disagree after applying the standard verification tests applicable to such empirical concepts. However, the same is not true with regard to the psychological, educational and epistemological concepts that are basic to liberation talk. Key to the understanding of the line of thought in this book is our understanding of how these psychological concepts mean and how they work.

I have already alluded to the fact that many conceptual puzzlements result from the *mis*-application of concepts. I shall make attempts at showing how we can begin to solve certain conceptual perplexities that result from such *mis*-taking or *mis*-application of key psychological concepts, all of the family used in liberation talk. This can be accomplished by looking at dispositional and activity words.

Dispositions Versus Activities

Understanding the distinction between activity words and dispositional words must be clarified and truly understood if this work is to make any sense whatever. As a matter of fact, its arguments are based on the fact that we have a tendency to *mis*-notice this key distinction as we mistake activity words for dispositional words, and so either continue to talk past each other, or *mis*-apply key concepts and lose the "life-changing aspects of the concepts" in the process.

In short, many fatal conceptual confusions result from our failure to make this simple, but significant distinction. We shall first look at some very familiar words and then move over to the word "liberation."

Many words like "know," "believe," "understand," and "aspire" point to dispositions people have rather than to activities they perform. The grammar of dispositional words is essentially different from the grammar of activity words. Gilbert Ryle captured this for us when he said:

> The verbs 'know,' 'possess' and 'aspire' (dispositional words) do not behave like the verbs 'run,' 'wake-up,' 'tingle.' We cannot say 'he knew so and so for two minutes, then stopped and started again after a breather,' he 'gradually aspired to be a bishop,' or 'he is now engaged in possessing a bicycle.'[5]

But, we can say that "he was digging for an hour, stopped for a breather, and then started to dig again." The distinction between *dispositional* words and *activity* words is much like the differences between the two types of ways of talking of which examples are given above. Many words used to describe human behavior are in fact dispositional words. Some combine dispositional and activity nuances.

Describing many of the words used to talk about human behavior as dispositional is a lively way of reviving the old myth of the ghost in the machine conceptualization for mind (psychological) concepts. It quietly carries with it aspects of the human will and does not leave man totally at the mercy of his environment as many modern thinkers would have us believe.

For while the seeing of these controlling concepts as dispositional and learned when one learns the language, we also discover that the same concepts have a way of controlling and governing lives and behaviors from within—aspects of the will, a classic notion that has been in hibernation for years now.

There is a logical grammar to dispositional words. A man may be described as truthful, but that does not mean that he is telling the truth at every moment of the day. If one is described as a pipe-smoker that does not mean that he is smoking his pipe at every moment of the day. To be described as a pipe-smoker means that one has the tendency, leaning or habit of smoking a pipe. The various acts of smoking the pipe and the overall "tendency to smoke" have different grammars.

The former is an activity or episode with a beginning, middle and end; it could be stopped and started again. The latter is a disposition, a character trait, a possession if you will, that expresses itself from time to time in the activity of pipe smoking. The phrase "to smoke a pipe" can be used in activity as well as dispositional descriptions.

This is the case because the phrase "to smoke" is dependent on the possibility of certain acts of smoking from time to time. But, both uses would be of different texture. Most dispositional words have correlated activities. Despite the many cases in which dispositional words correspond with episodic phrases, some dispositional phrases are highly generic and determinable, while others are highly specific.

For example, there is one key activity that correlates and counts in regard to being a pipe-smoker. But there are many activities correlated with greediness.

Most of the psychological (mind) concepts such as know, understand, and mastery are of the category labelled generic. In these, there is no one way of expressing the having of it. Rather, they express a crisscross of tendencies, abilities or a proneness to do things of lots of different kinds, never just one. Certain conceptual confusion will result when those who use dispositional words—liberate, understand, overcome etc.—think that there is but one metaphorical act that truly correlates.

Chapter Seven Notes

[1] Gilbert Ryle, "Taking Sides in Philosophy," in Collected Papers, Volume II, New York: Barnes and Noble, 1971, pp. 153-154.

[2] Ludwig Wittgenstein, Philosophical Investigations, Trans. G.E.M. Anscombe. New York: Macmillan and Company, 1968, Note 309.

[3] Gilbert Ryle developed the notion of mind as popularly seen as the ghost in the machine. He proceeds to analyze mind in order to show that mind is a concept with many sub-concepts, used to talk about human dispositions and activities. *The Concept of Mind*. New York: Barnes and Noble, 1949.

[4] Ryle, "Taking Sides in Philosophy," pp. 153-154.

[5] Gilbert Ryle, *Concept of Mind*, p. 116.

Chapter Eight

Liberation Is a Capacity Concept

Any serious look at a concept like liberation in general, and black liberation in particular, will require some analysis of the language that holds that concept, the form of life of the people who claim the language and have permission to use it, and the grammar or logical geography that controls, governs, and sets the limits of the language.

Another look at a concept like mind demonstrates that similar concepts could indeed be problematic and given to category mistakes. Liberation is one such concept that has been mangled and grossly mismanaged for political purposes.

I happen to believe that the depth revolutionary nuances of the word liberation have been missed as black and other Third World thinkers skirt the surface in their effort to score quick verbal and political points.

When it is discovered, after our analysis is complete, that liberation is not an activity or set of activities done in some process towards liberation, but is actually a *capacity/dispositional/mastery/achievement* word, we will all realize the need for acquiring true liberation.

This sets the stage for our doing all the liberating things (because we have the capacity, disposition and will) that are waiting to be done, but which could never be done by a timid people whose language and form of life together tell all with eyes to see what they will do some day.

THE OVERCOME

The message to all who listen is that "after we are liberated," "after we have overcome," we shall do it. But, in all our language, as I have said before, there is no success criteria, and none can declare and proclaim, because none will accept, that blacks have already been liberated not once, but several times through their own efforts. For some reason, as a people, they refuse to accept and declare it and persist in living in the "shall mood."

Key to our argument is the establishment of the distinction between activity words and dispositional words. A clarification and recall of this distinction must be made because many conceptual confusions of the type experienced by liberation thinkers result from this type of *mis*-noticing of the distinction between activity words and dispositional words.

Words like "know" and "understand" point to dispositions a person might have and not to activities. The grammar, or make-up and ruled functioning for dispositional words, is essentially different from the grammar of activity words. As Gilbert Ryle aptly relates:

> The verbs 'know,' 'possess' and 'aspire' (dispositional words) do not behave like the verbs 'run,' 'wake-up' or 'tingle.' We cannot say 'he knew so and so for two minutes, then stopped and started again after a breather,' 'he gradually aspired to be a bishop,' or 'he is now engaged in possessing a bicycle.'[1]

But, we can say, "He was digging for an hour, stopped for a breather and then started to dig again."

The distinction between activity and dispositional words is much like the two ways of talking of which examples have been given.

Now, many words used to describe human behavior are in fact dispositional words. Some combine dispositional and activity nuances. In such cases, only a careful heeding of the grammar of the word can determine its function. Describing many of the words used to talk about human behavior as dispositional is a lively substitute for the old myth of the "ghost in the machine"—that occult force which exerted energies that controlled and governed behavior. I dare say that such thinking must be re-introduced in the black liberation process.

For here, again, concepts that could be correlated to the human will, with powers to bring off certain things, are absent from the repertoire of functional concepts. In behaviorism, outside forces and circumstances of birth, skin color, environment or cultural deprivation, all negative stoppers, are used to convince contemporary blacks that outside forces have totally incapacitated them, taken away their powers of will, with all their capacities to effect liberating things.

As we go about the process of preparing for the taking charge of all aspects of our lives by declaring Overcome/Passover, we had better install, along with success/triumphalism, concepts about the "will," the innerman with its powers to bring things off against the odds.

The Logical Grammar or Geography of Dispositional Words

A man may be described as truthful, but that does not mean that he is somehow telling the truth at every moment of the day. If one is described as a pipe-smoker, that does not mean that one is smoking his pipe at every moment of the day. To be described as a pipe-smoker means that one has the tendency, leaning or habit of pipe smoking. The various acts or incidents of smoking the pipe, and the overall tendency to smoke have different grammars. The former, episodic moments of smoking the pipe, are activity related with clockable beginnings and ends. The latter, the tendency, is dispositional, pointing to a character trait or habit that from time to time expresses itself in the activity of smoking the pipe.

It should be noted here that the verb "to smoke" is dependent upon the possibility of certain acts of smoking from time to time. Consequently, one should note that some, indeed most, dispositional words have correlated and specific activities, such as *pipe-smoking* in which only one activity counts. While others, like *understand* are such that have no stock activity, but rather a family of activities that go with them. Such may signify a crisscross of tendencies, abilities, or "proneness to do not things of one unique kind, but things of lots of different kinds."[2] Overcome functions in similar ways.

THE OVERCOME

Imagine the conceptual confusion that could result when liberators and other conceptual change agents conclude that key dispositional or character concepts like liberation and overcome have but one metaphoric act that truly relates. Greater confusion results, however, from the tendency to see dispositional words as though they were activity words.

The inclination to misconstrue the nature of dispositional words is rampant. The description of dispositional words often contains elements of the potentiality-actuality controversy of classic philosophy. One can now see the tremendous powers for good lurking in our renewed understanding of how dispositional concepts interlock with appropriate activities, and how these get applied in the unfolding of the liberation of our people: potentiality/actuality.

Sugar has the potentiality to dissolve in water. It will always dissolve in water. But, dispositional words do not always work like this. A man may possess a truthful predisposition, but that does not mean that he is telling the truth all the time. There is no law-like necessity here as is true in the case of sugar dissolving in water. Again, aspects of the will, and other discriminating powers, must be brought to bear to control and govern the resulting activity.

Dispositional words alert one as to the abilities, liabilities, tendencies, propensities and capacities of a person. For example, in saying that a man knows French, one could conclude that he would react to, interpret, and understand conversations in French *anytime*, except of course if he is drugged, unconscious or currently deaf. The distinction between law-like dispositions and those of the more generic type must be made. For salt dissolves in water in a law-like manner, while most of the dispositions that are used to describe human competencies rarely function in this manner.

For human dispositions are not like animal instincts or human reflexes. These are gifts, innately given. Human instincts or reflexes are different at the core. Dispositions are learned propensities. Once learned, they carry with them aspects of "konnen"—can do, is able to do, ability to do this or that. To say that someone is a mathematician is to indicate that that person can do math. The problem is that the concept of "can" is used in such a rich variety of ways that tend to undermine or lessen the force of the German word, "konnen," as ability. Ryle captures the point for us when he says:

> 'Stones can float' (for pumice-stone floats); 'that fish can swim' (for it is not disabled, although it is now inert in the mud); 'John Doe can swim' (if he is willing to learn); 'you can swim' (when you try hard); 'she can swim' (because the doctor has withdrawn his veto).[3]

The "can" that is so often implied in the dispositional statements that are used to describe character is usually a learned ability that one has not yet forgotten, and which could be demonstrated from time to time in acts and episodes. "Can" expressions that picture or describe our character and dispositions point more often than not to the capacities and abilities which we have learned and acquired and not yet forgotten, and which we can authenticate by demonstrating from time to time in acts, behaviors and episodes. Liberation, seen as a dispositional word, will carry nuances of "can" pointing to our ability to bring off certain liberating things. Being liberated and mastering the family of liberation concepts then becomes prerequisite to and for doing the liberating thing.

The doing of the liberating thing then becomes dependent upon our stance and character—our capabilities and leanings—together with all the imperatives and commands inherent in living a liberated life. To contemplate this is not only radical but truly frightening.

For after acquiring the concept of liberation, one not only assumes the responsibility for today and tomorrow, but one goes further and understands that whatever it takes, whatever it costs, must be brought to bear on the situation if it is ever seen to be less than liberative. Herein begins real revolutions. People are prepared (like the first Christians) to die for the higher good—liberty in this context.

A sister concept of "can" is "tends." "Can" carries with it the nuance of certainty; "tends" carries the nuance of "more often than not," a reasonable bet that given certain conditions such and such behavior will be triggered.

THE OVERCOME

Tendencies interplay with the family of concepts that include "tastes," "habits," "bents," "leanings," and "hobbies."

The grammar of each is somewhat different. For example, a habit or act done from habit could be done apart from the conscious deliberation on the part of the actor. But, many other concepts, such as those pointing to discriminations and judgments, require that one "pays attention," "pays heed" or "attends what one is doing."

I again call attention to capacity concepts, reminding all that a capacity is demonstrated by the ability to produce, and produce consistently well, in accordance with the body of conventions established for the well-executed action or project. "To liberate" is a capacity verb and one of that very special sort that is used to signify that persons so described are now capably equipped to bring things off and get them right in a manner befitting a liberated person.

The Grammar of Mental Occurrences

Humans engage themselves in a variety of activities. They talk. They pray. They think. They eat. Some activities can be automatic, resulting from deeply inculcated habits. These are fine if the culture describes them as good and acceptable. There are some other activities that require aspects of "paying attention or attending what is being done." But, whatever else is applicable to activities, the governing paradigm of an activity, whether it be mental (like thinking) or physical (like digging), is that they must all have beginnings and endings in time.

One starts to think or talk and finishes sometimes. The same is true of praying and gardening. However, an activity like thinking can prove somewhat problematic. The start and finish of gardening can be easily recognized. This is not so in the case of thinking. There is no outward and visible sign that infallibly indicates that one has started to think or that one has stopped thinking. The knitted brow of concentration could be fake. It is often just that. Actors and hypocrites do that very well. But, the presence of some of the heed concepts (paying attention) can permit one to recount or narrate what one was thinking about.

Whether other minds could detect it or not, mental

activities, much like other activities, are clockable. They do have beginnings and endings—can be stopped and started again. On the other hand, dispositions, even when related to activity words, are never clockable. They are more like acquisitions or character traits that linger on and empower people to act and act correctly, by convention, over and over again.

Success or Achievement Words

Achievement or success words may resemble activity words. But, this resemblance can confuse. Therefore, it becomes important, once more, to make the distinction between "task verbs" and "achievement words." Task verbs predicate the activities involved in a given performance. A task verb is like the kicking of a soccer ball; and an achievement word, as it were, is that which records the scoring of the goal or point.

Achievements words can be seen as those words which crown the activities registered by task words in much the same way as reading (an activity) is crowned by understanding (a capacity). Task words point to the processes, while achievement words register the satisfactory (satisfactory convention or by the judgment of a referee or umpire) conclusion/completion of the task that was once in process, but is now complete.

In a very real sense, therefore, achievement words do not belong so much on the lips or in the mouth of the player, learner or actor, but on the lips of the umpire, teacher, educator, evaluator or the critical audience. For achievement words are used not to describe the many tryings in process, but the things gained after the many trials.

Hence, I might say that success implies that one has already overcome the obstacles in the way by victorious attempts at turning the "I can't do that" into the "I can do that, and I have already done that." The import of the word "konnen" reappears here. Our laborious attempt at demonstrating the difference between activity words and dispositional/capacity/achievement words is strategic to making the recurring point in this book.

Liberty, a dispositional/capacity/achievement word, must never be mistaken for liberative acts (demonstrations, protests, great speeches, etc.). These all have beginnings and endings in time.

They are perhaps required along the way to achieving liberty; they are definitely required after the achievement of liberty as signs that indicate that one is liberated. But, we must never mistake the one for the other. Should we do this, we should be making a major category mistake of the type that traps us into stringing one episode, one demonstration, one activity after another, all the time being very busy indeed, but never actually achieving, arriving or Overcoming—always on the way, but never arriving.

We might here consider the subtle distinction between task and activity words like "looking" and "trying" on the one hand and achievement words like "seeing" and "mastering" on the other hand. One can look (an activity), but seeing goes beyond looking and is of a different texture or grammar. Seeing does entail looking to a great degree, but to see something as different from other things requires more than simply the sense of sight. It also requires certain abilities and discriminating powers.

"Understanding" and "knowing" are somewhat like this. They, too, are character words. They are almost like states arrived at or achieved or possessed. Liberation fits into this mold also. One may note that we have already left off the mere talk about words and concepts and are actually dealing with human capabilities, powers and propensities. This happens with great ease—particularly when we are discussing psychological concepts—because soon we must leave the mere words and get to their essences, which happen to be people with concerns, dispositions and powers.

I have found these distinctions provided by Gilbert Ryle to be powerful analytical tools in managing the black liberation thought patterns. And, it is this that led me to see clearly that the failure in that enterprise is located just here as black thinkers miss the distinction between "try verbs" and "got it verbs" (mastered it), and as they go on forever pleading, blaming, crying, describing problems, but never claiming any victories and celebrating them and using them as the required breaks between periods of trying and the moments of achieving.

And so, black liberation thinkers are seen as they

remain engaged in a rich variety of "tryings" and activities. The problem is that verbs like "try" can be described by adjectives like "incorrect" or "erroneous"; achievement words like "know," "understand," "liberation" and "solve" cannot be thus described. Error can be part of the grammar of "try verbs" in a way it cannot be part of the grammar of achievement words.

Recognizing the difference between activity and dispositional words will remain key to understanding why it will be required in the black liberation process to declare success and achievement if we will not be forever engaged in a series of tryings with no crowning and lasting achievements that can in turn empower us to go on and do greater and better things.

We must graduate at some point. We must be promoted, and the certificate that separates the tryings in process from the changed status that permits one to go on must at some time be delivered (in ceremony) and framed. In time, it will be cited on the resumé and pointed to as proof of success at least at that stage.

Teaching and Learning

A look at teaching and learning as concepts that are closely related, yet different in grammar, in efforts to bring forth the point I make about the place for the tryings in the process to the achievement, will complete my effort in this area. This is an analogy that is essential to our understanding why we dare say that black liberation thinking is in the pre-liberation stage (the trying stage) before the achieving of the sought-after status.

Teaching has failed if the student has not been enabled at the end of the many planned exercises "to go on, on his own" to master a variety of similar and different circumstances. In making this claim, one is admitting that the point of teaching is resident in attempts to nurture in students the ability and capacity to surpass the drudgery of instruction and drill and progress to the stage at which they can for themselves and of themselves solve certain problems they discovered themselves or that are laid upon them.

After teaching a boy to count from 1 to 100, he might be able to figure/calculate a variety of numeral variations even beyond 100. One may make the further step and liken teaching to grammar. There are few people for whom grammar is an end in and of itself. People learn the rules of grammar, not so much that they may become grammarians, but rather so that they can go on to speak grammatically.

There is a way of teaching grammar by rote until the key principles are truly inculcated. But, there is also that sense in which one might say that the grammar, once learned, is thereafter subsumed in the practices of speaking grammatically.

Teaching in this sense is like grammar, and speaking grammatically is a special competency or capability of some persons. Those who lack it also lack a skill and are consequently without the ability to speak grammatically. As Ryle states the issue:

> In ordinary life, as well as in the special business of teaching, we are much more concerned with people's competencies than with their cognitive repertoires, with the operations rather than with the truths that they learn. Indeed, even when we are concerned with their intellectual excellences and deficiencies, we are interested less in the stocks of truths that they acquire and retain than in their capacities to find out truths for themselves and their ability to organize and exploit them when discovered.[4]

Teaching, when described thus, becomes the preliminary task or activity and a means to the learning-mastery of given techniques.

Mastery as used above carries all the nuances of dispositional words that point to human capacities, abilities and propensities. I suggest again that teaching is activity-oriented. It has all the qualities of activities and fits the paradigm with beginnings and endings, with the possibility of interruption and restart. A class can be taught for an hour, a week or a semester. It can be interrupted intermittently and restarted at will.

If teaching occasions learning, however, the student's character changes. He/she acquires yet another capability and the enabling powers that correlate with it. One may not be able to pinpoint the moment at which teaching, the external activity of the second party, is transformed into learning. It may come suddenly as in a flash or gradually. But, whenever it happens, the learner assumes a new status. At this stage, because of his new possession, he can become a teacher of himself and of others.

Again, the likening of the intricate process to what happens when the student being taught grammar suddenly or gradually begins to speak grammatically is still the best analogy of which I can think. And, in many key ways, the liberation process of blacks will need something of this nature to occur, and the teaching/learning paradigm has much to offer in terms of the analysis.

The picture of the transformation process as that analogous to the teaching of grammar and then speaking grammatically offers the picture I see of the efficacious liberative black process.

I am suggesting that the learning of the thing that is taught through involvement of certain activities is signalled by the acquisition of yet another power, ability or competency. And, liberation is also about powers, competencies and abilities to effect liberative things in one's life.

A drastic mistake is made when we liken the liberative acts to liberation. This is tantamount to conceiving learning (a dispositional word) as an activity word. Rote teaching/learning could be like this, but it never permits the student to go on to, say, recite poetry with understanding, let alone create his own poetry.

Soren Kierkegaard, the Danish philosopher and theologian, speaks ably to the point within the context of discussing moral upbringing. In upbringing, the imparting of rote knowledge is never considered as the most basic thing in the learning process. He contrasts "merely getting to know something" with real upbringing and training. He says:

> Therefore the rule for the method in upbringing is that the one who is being brought up does as well as he can at every moment. Confusion arises when the upbringer instead of upbringing teaches as if he were imparting knowledge. It becomes sophistry when one thinks; what good is it for me to do it now since I am doing it poor-

ly; I must first get to know more, etc., but this is nothing but escapism and heresy. The rule is to do it as well as one can at every moment, and so on further, in order continually to get to know it better and better. If on the other hand, the upbringing is communicated as knowledge, one never receives an upbringing, but is always getting merely something to know.[5]

Kierkegaard's thinking in this area is closely related to that of Ryle and offers some further pointers as to the "how" of introducing students to new knowledge (concepts and competency) and new ways of seeing and doing in the world. This must be done by training, for Ryle, and upbringing for Kierkegaard. The rule for training and upbringing we have already noted is very similar to the rules that govern the teaching of the flute, grammar or karate.

The beginning rules must get applied in the very initial learnings, the first practicing through which the aspects of "knowing that" and "knowing how" get merged in the acquisition of a new competency that enables one not only to say that "I know," but also that "I can teach you and show you how, because I have already done it."

So, even though some amount of knowledge must be communicated in order to help those being introduced into the new way of seeing and doing master the task at hand (like the rote reciting of the rules before the applying of them), the rules must soon be taken up in the practices of upbringing, training, if the forming of life is to become the end result.

If the end is simply a good sermon or speech, then black liberators have indeed done a masterful job. If, however, the task is one of "forming liberated lives equipped to take charge of their own futures," then, "the instruction, communication, must not be as of knowledge, but upbringing, practicing, art-instruction."[6]

The "teaching of capability" is the terminology Kierkegaard uses to handle the issues under consideration here. Hence he states:

The rule for the communication of capability is: begin immediately to do it. If the learner says: I can't, the teacher answers: Nonsense, do it as well as you can. With that the instruction begins. Its end result: to be able, but it is not knowledge which is communicated. Rather it is capability that is communicated.[7]

The emphasis that is fundamental to any type of preaching, teaching or communication aimed at changing lives, young and old, is that what is to be effectively communicated is never more knowledge about things and circumstances and situations ("knowing that" in an about mood), but rather the transferring of competence or ability.

Kierkegaard recommends that instead of seeing the upbringing enterprise as a series of activities through which more facts are "banked" and more information imparted by the "pounding" the same into the heads of people through whatever communication methods (preaching, teaching), the teaching of capability requires an effective reversal of that process, "the pounding out" of the facts as they get applied in correct behaviors and activities.

For black liberators and change agents (preachers etc.) to think that their work is done at what is actually the very preliminary stage of outlining the facts about the plight of the black person in America and the larger world is terribly "incapacitating." It lacks what it takes to enable, being void of the capacities necessary in making the complicated moves required of people who know how to live significantly redeemed and changed lives.

In this, the importance of the teaching of concepts comes to the fore once more, pregnant with issues that remind us that the communication of ability to master (overcome) is most important in these areas of thinking.

When the eternal pessimists that comment on the black situation declare that our efforts are essentially time-wasting, I shudder. They are right to a point for *Nobody Can Teach Anyone Anything.* This title to a little book by W.R. Weis is suggestive of the issue. We can teach as much as we would, others must do the learning. But, in the black community, all are talking and no one is listening. Each can become his own preacher/teacher with his own private message. And there is no central message or story.

If the saying of the thing (describing it) continues to be the chief work of the change agent; if blacks are not forever to see themselves as passive beings waiting to have more and more things "done" to and for them by the powers that be; if the grievous conditions present in the environment are not to be seen as totally controlling in the "learning process," then at some point we must realize that the teacher (initiator) cannot originate creativity and response in the initiated.

The grammar of having mastered (overcome) something dictates and requires the presence of the initiated's own involvement, participation—in the process. The student himself must do something, even if it means simply attending what is being done. For as Ryle says:

> Where there is a modicum of alacrity, interest or anyhow docility in the pupil, where he tries however faintheartedly to get things right rather than wrong, fast rather than slow, neat rather than awkward, where, even, he registers even a slight contempt for the poor performance of others or chagrin at his own, pleasure at his own successes and envy at those of others, then he is, in however slight a degree, co-operating and so self-moving. He is doing something, though very likely not much, and not merely having things done to him.[8]

In other words, there must be some level of participation on the part of those who are to be led to develop "mastery" over whatever. They must show some eagerness or interest. Eagerness and desire to overcome or passover the "stoppers" are absolutely essential. But a host of capabilities and interest must be pooled for the acquisition of the mastery over the techniques that are to be communicated. These include methods, knacks and tricks of the "Overcoming/mastery" trade as well as the shortcuts and pitfalls.

If Ryle is correct, and I believe that he is, then would-be change agents (teachers, preachers, liberationists) should go about the business of offering hints on rules of procedure, methods and modus operandi. For those they seek to liberate or teach can register success only when they can make for and of themselves essentially new and novel moves using the acquired redemptive techniques.

Again, their work becomes more like what teachers of grammar do: impart rules and methods of procedure. The test is in speaking grammatically. For the liberationist, the test of success is living the liberated life. Methods, not facts, are what blacks need. "A method being a learnable way of doing something."[9]

I am here reminded that there is something of a public character in rules and methods. They can be common to all and followed by all. But generally, there are a multiplicity of things that can be done by following the one method. This is generally the case because methods offer guidelines for performing certain tasks.

In ways it could be said that they hold the "do's and don't's" related to the procedure at hand. In fact, this is all the "change agent" or teacher can offer. The initiated/students must themselves learn to make the connections. This they do by practice. I dare say that apart from the practicing of the rules of liberation (taking charge, building institutions, learning to value, pass-on tradition, interpret using common starting points like the black Overcoming/Passover, etc.), the black situation will remain one that could be likened to our having given blacks ropes with which they hang or beat themselves, rather than skip.

On the other hand, change agents, teachers and preachers can only give the people the ropes and the rules of skipping. They must of and for themselves begin the exercise of skipping. No one can do that for them. Once blacks learn this key lesson, the eager ones can indeed seek out the rules for putting together successful and liberated lives.

The reader is reminded once more, to the point of redundancy, that the contrasting of teaching and learning and activities and dispositions carries the secret of black redemption that cannot be taken away. There are some very important things in our lives which can be measured by time.

According to our paradigm, these are activities. They are important. We do them; we must do them. What preachers, teachers and liberation fighters do is activity-based. They are either doing these things or they are not. But, there are some other very key concepts, some pointing to character, dispositions and capabilities, understanding, mastery and liberation that cannot be measured in time. They are dispositional words.

So, it remains true that success can be registered only when the varied activities used in teaching or communicating succeed somehow in transforming persons so that they can acquire the capacities required to continue and progress on their own, making essentially independent moves along the way. For to have learned something is neither an activity nor a task. It is the achievement of a new possession that changes the character and consequently the powers of the learner. Teaching can only set the stage for learning. The former is task-oriented. The latter is dispositionally-oriented. And, yet they are very closely related concepts.

Success Criteria

What can count as criteria for having mastered a given issue? For example, if we have been taught how to use certain concepts by our teachers, what criteria can that teacher use to validate the claim that the student has mastered the concepts? We certainly cannot do this by pointing to brainwaves. A teacher has simple ways of making such determination, being aware as he/she is of the fact that criteria are those public signs, taken from the shared form of life with its vast body of conventions governing rules of success, which can be used to indicate that one has indeed mastered the issue.

I believe that the criteria for having mastered an issue or tasks are evidenced in what a person is "able to do and say." There are certain activities and features—doings, sayings and showings—which the conventions of the form of life accept as normative, and which people initiated into that form of life and culture all share. These in turn become public signs of mastery.

The contention here seems to support certain theories commonly labelled behaviorism. For it appears as though we are advocating and advancing the doctrine that mastery is determinable by means of an examination of the outward and public behaviors of humans. But such could not be our final conclusion.

In fact, in these matters, we never seek any final conclusion. Such is presumptuous, for at any time another language game could be brought into play offering another workable way of seeing and doing. But that is not our main difficulty with behaviorism which uses behavior as the final criterion for determining things. The main problem is that this type of behaviorism is quite unable to give adequate account of the hoaxes—like play acting, mimicking and pretending.

Norman Malcolm stated the issue well for us. He says, "My criteria for one's being in pain is, first, his behavior and circumstances, and second, his words (often they have been found to be connected in the right way with his behavior and circumstances)."[10]

So, success criteria are made up of the sum total of characteristic and recognizable features, embedded in, and defined by, the conventions of a given form of life. They are also identified in the same way as the conventions are identified. It should be obvious that the living conventions are bound up with the fundamental concept, form of life, which is the first cause and prime mover in this type of philosophizing.

Any attempt to challenge the criteria offered by the form of life and operative body of conventions sets the stage for the development of a private or "revolutionary new language." When an appeal is made to the form of life, we appeal to the final arbitrator—the body of operating conventions.

Chapter Eight Notes

[1] Gilbert Ryle, "*Concept of Mind*," p. 116.

[2] Ibid., p. 118.

[3] Ibid., pp. 126-127.

[4] Ibid., p. 28.

[5] Soren Kierkegaard, "Journals and Papers," Vol. 1, A-E, edited and translated by Howard V. Hong and Edna H. Hong. Bloomington: Indiana University Press, 1967, p. 279.

[6] Ibid., pp. 279-280.

[7] Ibid., p. 284.

[8] Gilbert Ryle, "Teaching and Training" in Collected papers, Volume II, pp. 451-464.

[9] Ibid., p. 460.

[10] Norman Malcolm, "Wittgenstein's Philosophical Investigations" in Wittgenstein and the "Problem of Other Minds," edited by Harold Morick, New York: McGraw-Hill, 1967, pp. 24-25.

Chapter Nine

Language, Form of Life, And Black Conventions

This chapter is begun by claiming that linguistic forms must be merged with human capacities and activities. There is a compounding of human activities and life circumstances with a miscellany of wishes, hopes, intentions, levels of seriousness, capabilities and insufficiencies, all coming together in another metaphor, often used by Wittgenstein, "form of life."

There is a sense in which the form of life, in this case, black pre-liberation form of life, existing in the "shall someday mode," colors all articulation. This is colored to such a degree that ready indications of what is intended by any statement coming off the lips of one living in such a form of life is shown more forcefully from the form itself than from the words. The pre-liberation form of life in which black Americans find themselves today frames and governs black life, and colors its language in such a way as to entrap them.

In many cases words require this matrix of a "form of life" as necessary and prerequisite to the gathering of sense from the sayings. In other words, what is said must often be interpreted in conjunction with the total picture of the person's character—qualities, capacities, tendencies—in short the person's total psychological and behavioral make-up. The consequence is that a person's (more appropriately to our purpose, a people's) practices, deeds and character must hang with the words uttered if sense is to be made of what has been said.

THE OVERCOME

There is a complex of conventions, grammar and form of life, like culture, which must pour light on language. A form of life, for our purposes, can best be described as that governing complex of language, with attendant moods, ethos or dominating way of "looking at and intending" in the world. The form of life, and the language that goes with it, have a strange way of both qualifying and limiting the individuals who exist within that form and language. This means that the rules and criteria for judging one form of life may not be applicable in another, for the standard of judgment, what is important, may not be identical. But, within the form of life, the given body of conventions, issue the judgment criteria.

This analysis shows how a given form of life, pre-liberation form of life for blacks the world over, traps them in a double whammy, by language and by conventions. It also explains why even the sharpest black liberation thinkers are themselves trapped in this pre-liberation stage by language and conventions.

One strange phenomenon existent within the black form of life is the tendency to believe and act as though the simple "saying" of a thing makes it real. The black preacher preaches, and it is finished. The black Christian "prays," and it is finished. The saying seems to be always sufficient. To my mind, only of the God of Genesis can it be said: "He spake and it was done." This strange belief that words and the saying of things—apart from concerted efforts to institutionalize, thereby incorporating the new thing into the body of conventions—are considered enough, is that which causes hesitation when I call for the black Overcome. Is it possible that black thinkers believe that because blacks for the most part act as though the saying of it is the doing of it, the only hoped for result would be a linguistic Passover whereby we simply change the lyrics of a song and fall back into the trap of praying without effecting prayer within the context of the faith that generated the prayer?

There can be no Passover without going the extra required steps of "walking into the future" with basic rules for a ruled life, with fundamental covenants which cannot be contravened without real consequences, and with a commitment to build from the ground up, if needs be, the life-saving and enhancing institutions that will give life to the newly developed way of seeing within the growing body of conventions that shape and govern in due turn the form of life and the new and old language.

The proper way of viewing "proclamation," the saying of the thing, is not by believing that by saying it is done, but recognizing that saying, like praying, sets the conceptual stage for instituting; that is, adding new abiding concepts and life-saving institutions to the body of the existing conventions. So words cannot hang loose in a fashion detached from the speaker's life. A showing must accompany the saying of human communication. The showing and the saying are to be integrated in at least two ways—in the grammar, the speaking grammatically and in the form of life.

There is much in this point for black liberation thinkers. It reminds us that human lives are tied up in a mix of activities of telling and showing. Since the black liberator's chief business has to do with new ways of seeing and doing in the world, with how future lives are formed in a liberative mood, it must take seriously our considerations about levels of caring, ways of hoping and intending in the world and forms of life.

It has, therefore, the task of at least nurturing those who are to be the subjects of liberation to the point of understanding the true nature of liberation—Overcome—and not as only a statement, but as a new status that one has gained the capacities, propensities and masteries necessary to hope, speak, and institute into the body of conventions the new conceptions with their institutional consequences.

The form of life, therefore, entails much of what I would like to label the "non-linguistic extras." Here again, the black liberator must take account of this revelation. For the development of the capacities that make the above possible through the process of mastering concepts, the indicative as well as the imperative aspects of concepts, seems to be one of the better descriptions of the task of the liberation thinker.

Now, the way of becoming acquainted with a form of life is similar to the way one in which one gets attuned to the waves and moods of a culture. It entails the development of the competencies to identify the totality of dispositions, capacities, hopes, fears, and intentions that are normative within the black form of life and consistent with the high water marks of the culture's ideology.

One of the problems in the black form of life is its tendency not to identify high water marks, corporate successes, which can become the basis for forming the controlling, overriding ideology through which at least "I can do it" because real or mythological forbears under worse circumstances did it.

For in a real sense, the ideological umbrella that shelters a given form of life helps to shape and keep in perspective just what are the legitimate hopes and fears, dispositions and intentions to be blessed by the culture. It is precisely in this "formative" area that black liberation theology must step out of the mind-set, the current language and form of life and establish the page-break with the negative, self-destructive and dysfunctional aspects of the language and culture.

This theology must declare its Overcome, and from the vantage point of having overcome linguistic and conceptual slavery, engage in the creation of a new set of concepts dealing with Overcoming, with their correlated institutional rites and structures which must be quickly added to the existent body of conventions. But not just as another add on. There have been enough of those.

The future classification of the total black experience will then be codified as *the before/and after.* Before we experienced and accepted our liberating/exalting event, such and such was the way of seeing, hoping, and intending in our world. But now that we have identified, accepted and gladly celebrate our Overcoming/liberating/exalting event, we think and do in such and such different ways. We conceive new concepts, we share them, and we find ways to institute them, making them a part of the abiding body of conventions which will be passed on to our children and our children's children.

I think that we are on the right track in looking at language and form of life. I think that the success criteria that are lacking from the black form of life must be added and exalted as a prerequisite for living within a liberated form of life with its attendant liberating language.

If we are right, and if language as human activity gets placed in a form of life or culture that gives it point and meaning; if the current state of affairs within the form of

A BLACK PASSOVER

life experienced by blacks the world over is lacking in key areas such as those which could be likened to the Jewish Passover, circumcision rites, and other rites of passage; and if we are forced to declare that the criteria for judging and the historic or mythical samples of victories as a people are non-existent, then the first task is one of garnering from the total experience those moments of victory. This means those events through which the oppressed blacks have already demonstrated their competency to be victorious, and carve these so that they become a permanent part of the body of informative conventions.

The first task is to get the conventions of the form of life in order and in shape to do its silent work. The form of life, since it is to become the over-riding non-spoken grammar, with the final unwritten rules for deciding and umpiring within the culture, must be equipped to handle all aspects of a liberated people with permission to talk, build and critique.

The form of life for the liberated must therefore be built up to include all necessary concepts and rules of operation for a liberated people, and the liberation thinker must be involved actively in this process. There must be aspects of creating new concepts and institutional rites and liturgies to make sure that the culture can answer all its questions. So far, liberation thinkers have been very good at describing issues and problems for which there are no answers in the culture even with its interpretive body of conventions.

Embarrassingly missing, as we have stated before and will state again, are pointers to what can count as success criteria, what must be in place before declaring the Overcoming/Passover of our people and there through establishing the necessary page break with the past way of thinking and doing.

This way of tying language to form of life is not unlike what the French existentialists once advocated as they saw individuals with all their activities (including linguistic ones) as rooted and grounded in the context of their cultures, inclusive of customs, morals, beliefs, hopes, fears, system of judgment, and ideologies. Because the culture traps us, we are virtually in need of an extra-culture, brand new way of devising the exit from the trap, one that I believe is chiefly a conceptual trap.

THE OVERCOME

Our hopes, fears, beliefs and so on are all learned when we learn the concepts of our language. And if in those learnings are nowhere to be found concepts that deal with corporate Overcoming, with success criteria, no wonder that even old men and women in the black race go to their graves hoping through their song that they will Overcome someday.

The black liberation thinker who must pass on a sense of liberation to future generations, on discovering that many key concepts are indeed absent from the culture, must busy himself with creating the new concepts and passing them on, recognizing that a powerful role is played by learned or acquired concepts in forming, framing and governing lives.

But alas, many black thinkers believe like B.F. Skinner, and others of his persuasion, that the environment alone shapes and forms lives. This is the passive way of looking at things. It is done for and upon us. Part of the logical grammar of liberation points to the fact that liberation ought not to be done for us. In that way it can never become "our competency, capacity or disposition." This we must do for ourselves, even if we allow others to show us the way. Even if we appropriate types and concepts from others, until they are truly appropriated, made our own, the cycle is not complete.

On the Grammatical

I dared to say that this work wants very much to offer a grammar for managing the doing of liberation thinking in the black key. Without doubt, this is a presumptuous task. We shall therefore take a moment to examine the concept of grammar as it is applied here, in order that it could be understood when used here subsequently.

Grammar is that which governs the proper use of language. But, in our way of using the word, it means much more than the analyzing and parsing of verbs, etc. Grammar includes much more than this. It includes the speaker's life, his motives, his natural habitat if you will. In a sense, grammar, as used by the masters of conceptual analysis, is used to point roughly to what others call culture, and I often call body of conventions. For it is really in the culture that permissible ways of using language are located. So language, in order to mean, must be grounded in a person's total life and culture. (Note how I love to use the flag words, body of conventions!)

The grammar of a word/concept includes, not only the personality and life of the person behind the words, but also all the permissible stock and nonstock usages for that word as authorized by the culture (operative conventions). The grammar of a word would therefore give descriptive insight into the very essence of the concept. The one supports the other, offering acceptable and interpretive form that compounds to aid understanding and meaningfulness.

Another way of viewing the concept of grammar is that in which it is likened to the traditional categories, those basic and very general facts about nature and life that cannot be intelligently denied. These very general and basic facts of life are there, as it were, as common furniture for all to use. They include the fact that the world is; that I am, that air exists though unseen. These claims are not up for argumentation or given to dispute. They are there, like the tangible *apriori* simples of daily life and talk. Grammar appeals to this foundation for meaning, for form and for authority. Concepts are made meaningful when their grammar is consistent with the world.

Remember, always, that the grammar of a word includes that body of conventions, the categories, definitions, stock and non-stock usages as well as the language game or linguistic context that "hang" with the word. To state this contention differently, one can say that a concept is useless only when in the entire world we can find no grammar that can fit its use.

Generally, only madmen and children who are still learning to speak, or sick men recovering from brain strokes, use language with no regard to depth grammar. For grammar is like the non-linguistic essence of the word which tells quietly all that is entailed, all that is ingredient and all the possible usages and meanings which are consistent with making that word or concept function.

Now, children are taught grammar in their language lessons at school. They are taught how words fit properly into sentences. But if all that they have learned is this superficial grammar, then the teacher has failed miserably. For the intent was to train them how to speak grammatically.

When, therefore, we speak of grammar, we are not simply referring to the arrangement of words in sentences. This is so, because as has already been indicated, grammar has a way of telling the entire truth about a concept. Grammar can tell us about our world. By way of aside, there is even a grammar that permits people to tell lies and others to discover the lie.

The warning must therefore be made, lest we tend to continue to mistake a grammatical play for something else by taking some sayings as though they were descriptive of physical phenomena. In short, we remind ourselves that the grammar of a word serves as that non-linguistic core which cannot be violated. And yet, within the limits of usage consistent with the grammar of a word or concept, there can be a wide range of applications within human mouths and language games.

This key notion of grammar is absolutely essential to my analysis, because, in cases where the special words I will use have no locale on the lips or in the mouths of blacks; no connection yet with the dreamed for, perceived reality that is yet to be; no referent in real life if you will, in such cases, the grammar of the word must stand alone and do the initial work that permits us to elevate, in time, the other aspects of the concept into the conventions of the people to function efficaciously in the future.

When one considers that certain words like "mermaids and unicorns" have a grammar that precludes the location of referents, one quickly realizes that other ways of taking such concepts must be sought. In like manner (never to lose the opportunity) when we introduce a concept like the black "Overcoming/Passover event" with no referent in the current body of conventions (until I put it there, like Churchill or President Johnson making words like de-escalating and making us all use them to talk about states of affairs thereafter), only the grammar of the word would permit its initial use at this stage. In the contemplation of these issues, we soon discover that different grammars permit referring, fictitious, factual, poetic, mythological, and so on, uses of language.

And the language and form of life followed (like culture) carries with it, embodies in a dynamic sense, the grammar that permits people to understand it. People, following the same form of life can usually, and with great ease, grasp the point. They easily understand, mainly because they corporately see the world in the same fashion as described by the grammar of their common language.

Grammar, therefore, will be used to point to the nonlinguistic extras that help to frame and limit concepts, making them meaningful. For there is often a relationship, though not necessarily one to one, between some concepts and the world. But, there are instances when such is not the case. And it is in such instances that "grammar" is called upon to tell what kind of an object a thing is. So we speak of "mermaid," and "Excalibur" and "overcome"; and they can mean and mean effectively in context, and if they are never asked to do more than the language permits them to do.

So, "grammar" can offer some extra information on facts, states of affairs and objects in the world. But "grammar" can also signal and indicate whether a word has fictitious, emotive, legendary, mythical, scientific or conditional connotations. It is used in our work to tell a wide range of things about words and concepts.

Take as an example the following: Can a machine have a toothache? The answer cannot issue from past experience. Neither can it come from an examination of the peculiar machine. The answer comes, rather, from the grammar of the word machine. One can say that the above is indeed an unconventional way of speaking about machines. And in current common parlance, the conventions, together with the grammar of the word machine, tells that machines cannot feel pain. And no empirical testing is necessary either. The final and acceptable answer to the question posed comes from the grammar regulating the use of the word machine in sentences and questions.

And it is enough. In like manner, the grammar of the word "pain" and the word "toothache" tells that they cannot fit machines. As a result, in the entire world, with its multiplicity of language games, with stock and non-stock usages, nothing can count as the case of machines experiencing pain from toothache. Grammar, you will see, has the unique job within our system for establishing the placing of our concepts in meaningful combinations within our language. And through this process, it governs the relevance of statements, questions and sighs and quietly determines their relevance to the concepts at hand.

And so, we see grammar relating the concept of a chair to several other concepts like, sitting, mending and breaking. A chair soon becomes something that humans (and monkeys) can sit on, can break or mend, though mending in a different way from that in which a man is asked to mend his old, evil ways. This procedure, far as it is from the central purpose of this work (it would appear), demonstrates the importance of separating concepts from mere names that label things.

Naming gives the impression that singularity of application is the norm, while concepts anticipate the necessary overlap and crisscross of nuances. The point is that there are several types of relationships between concepts, the world and other concepts which the linguistic grammar of which we now speak, generated by the conventions and form of life, establish and maintain.

There is yet another way of seeing grammar. It could be seen as that which, although itself non-linguistic, offers a form and a frame for words and concepts within a language.

And in some cases, words simply make no sense apart from the form (grammar) they assume. To demonstrate that sense does not come from words alone, one need only look at how the same words can mean differently within different language games or contexts. Consider the differences between the indicative, imperative, interrogative and conditional forms of expressions that may actually use the very same words. Very similar arrangements of words can mean differently in each case, and only the form can account for the point/meaning intended.

In these cases, the form is not spoken. The form must rather be shown. The form is there, as it were, mirrored in the language. This is why I believe that black liberation thinkers fail their people by offering a language with no redemptive forms from the culture; no set of chalked-up winnings, banked in the culture (like the old doctrine of supererogation) to be relied on as grammatical support for the linguistic saying of some key things in liberation talk.

Wittgenstein, the father of this method, was fond of

comparing theologizing and philosophizing with grammar. In other words, what philosophers and theologians do is very much like what grammarians and logicians do. Students are taught grammar so that they could go beyond the initial memorization of the rules (facts) to the point where, with a degree of ease, they can begin to speak grammatically.

Hence, grammar is never an end in itself, but a means to a greater end, that of achieving a new status, with acquired competencies that permit grammatical speaking. The same must be true for the theologian of liberation. He must somehow move his reader to the point of mastery, where he lives and talks and sings and hopes in the mood and from the state (status) of the liberated.

The redemptive trick in all this procedure is that which leads us to discover that as in the case of learning grammar to speak grammatically, so in the case of acquiring concepts appropriate to liberation. The stage is set for claiming that as the rules of grammar get merged into the activity of speaking grammatically, so too the rules of liberation, laid bare through conceptual analysis, set the stage for the merging of the rules and concepts into the living of the liberated life.

The liberator, the change agent, must realize at every step of the way that what he does is very much like what the grammarians are asked to do and never an end in itself, but a means to a greater end: transformed status with the powers to become and function as befits the liberated person.

Form of Life

I indicated earlier that the meaning of concepts are tied to a complex of conventions, grammar and the form of life followed. Because of this interrelationship, the meaning of a given word cannot be always clearly and simply stated.

And often, an accompaniment from the life followed (lived) is sometimes absolutely necessary for full understanding. For what the signs in a language fail to express verbally, the life can show. This is one of the ways through which we discover the sincerity of people and the degree of seriousness to their formal statements. As Paul

THE OVERCOME

Holmer indicates:

> the same sentence may be truth in one person's mouth and a falsehood in another not because of anything like 'relativism' or because of a radical subjectivity, but rather because words are never true simply as words. They need mouths, persons, situations and the right context, even the right feelings, emotions and passions to go with them. All of this is part of the non-linguistic that will frequently have to be shown to you, to be seen by you, before the word or words make sense.[1]

The line of argument followed here forces upon us the consideration of the importance of the "form of life" followed. I am myself convinced that the failure of the black liberation thinkers to effect change after all the good writing and speaking that has already being accomplished, can be attributed to the quality of the form of life that has been lived in black communities. Neither the language nor the life, for the most part, germinates the kind of concepts, the examples of victories or the confidence in even the ability to effect change. There is a woeful absence from the culture (form of life) of blacks of some key ingredients. And these must be corporately installed before we can effectively go further.

What I am getting at, stated in another fashion, reminds us that a "form of life" is dependent upon the kind and quality of human consciousness; that is, human ways of caring in a world with many possibilities for victories as well as failures. And just as one man has the ability to use a word in many different ways, so a man may be able to intend the world and care in the world in different ways. But he must always do his caring and intending of the world within the framework of the form of life that limits and qualifies him.

And herein lies my greatest fear for the true liberation of my people. They grapple with a language and dominant form of life, with no stories, myths, instances of Overcoming through heroes or battles won.

They contend with a form of life, described forever and always in negatives terms; with a form of life with

A BLACK PASSOVER

only an impossible "Vision Glorious" walking hand in hand in Martin Luther King's conceptualization, or as a black nation within a nation, as Malcolm X preached,—a form of life fed only by negatives which can only develop a language and culture full of negatives, conceptual as well as behavioral. So they think, sing, talk, walk and live. And the truly frightening aspect of this situation is our knowing that both the "form of life followed" and the language spoken, limit and qualify, and in the case of blacks, trap.

Blacks will need, I suspect, to install into the language and form of life of blacks, key victory and achievement concepts. If they are not actually there resident in the culture, then aspects of our history must be redone in such a way as to create identifiable moments of victory, identifiable heroes, and easy to tell and remember stories about how they "Overcame" this or that would-be stopper.

And, after recognizing that individuals have Overcome, the culture of black Americans must next corporately install the one event/moment through which they all declare corporate victory over the negative forces that are stopping them from achieving.

The formal strategic intention of this book is simply to demonstrate from a variety of standpoints the absolute necessity for us, as black people, to install in the language and culture, the concept of Overcome/Passover, as a prerequisite for granting the language and culture the capability of speaking and showing using the Overcome concept.

For if the concepts of a language are that through which the culture communicates, the means through which lives are formed, it should be obvious that certain aspects of liberation, absent as they are from the language (with no concepts of victory, triumph, celebration for accomplishment), and with no myths or heroes (no David who killed 10,000; no King Arthur and Round Table; no Waterloo; no Fourth of July; no Passover); then it will be no wonder that blacks remain conceptually trapped. The real initial work has not yet been done.

The event has been "given," for we already have the ready-made moment, man and story, but we have not yet found the way to corporately turn this God-sent event into the Overcoming/Passover event. Then we must install it in the culture and language, so that it can in turn form lives as our children feed on it and as the society takes on the task of nurturing the capabilities, propensities, and abilities that must accompany the introduction of the "Overcome concept." This will in turn permit (make possible) our people to look at their world, think, do, care, hope, intend and institute in their world in the "Overcome" way.

The introduction of the concept "form of life" reminds us that words cannot hang loose in a fashion of detachment from the speaker's life. The net result is that they integrate and crisscross with human life that must be summoned if the utterances are to mean. Once more, the saying and showing (language and accompanying form of life) aspects of total human communication reappear.

The showing and the saying are indeed integrated in at least two ways, in the grammar, speaking grammatically and in the form of life. There is much in this for black leaders and change agents to contemplate. It shows that human lives are tied up in activities of not only "telling," but also in "showing." What is shown can more effectively communicate than what is told. A "saying" is always included in the showing.

And if our chief business at this stage of black development has to do with how liberated lives are formed, we must take into account our consideration of our levels of caring, seeing and intending, and how these are infused from the language and the body of conventions. And if some of the key ingredients are missing from the body of informative conventions and from the stock of life-changing concepts of the language, then we *must* first install them.

And if you doubt that such can be installed, remember what Churchill and President Johnson did; and remember Kwanza and animal rights and homosexual rights.

The form of life, therefore, entails much of what we have elsewhere called the non-linguistic plus. This is one's way of seeing and intending, of judging and describing, of evaluating and discriminating between the important that merit attention, the not so important, and downright garbage. And throughout, we must always remember that the development of the capacities that will make the above possible, through the process of mastering from the culture and language the key liberation concepts, with their prescriptive, indicative, and imperative aspects all intact, is prerequisite to Overcoming.

The one danger in this entire process is the fact that some of these concepts are not yet installed in the culture and language and must be before the black liberation thinkers can move off base. If they have been wondering with the preachers and others why after 20 years so little progress, they should think again about these things. They should look again, not at any new facts, but with a new perspective for viewing the extant facts. And they (we) *must* install triumphalism and victory and the Overcome as done deals through past individuals whose work and integrity we will not question, but simply accept.

That we have not yet done this is also a sign of our pre-liberation status. We may be feeling that we have no authority to do this thing. But we had better give ourselves that authority, today, as we engage in prime cultural development—installing the needed concepts on liberation (as done deal) and on success criteria, so that in turn, they could be used to inform, govern and shame us if our language thereafter and our behavior/actions do not match that new positive imagery, the Overcome language and culture will force upon us.

The way of becoming acquainted with a form of life (the redeemed, Overcome/Passover form of life) is somewhat similar, if not identical, to the way in which one gets attuned to the waves and mood of a culture. It entails the development of the competencies to identify the totality of dispositions, capacities, hopes, fears, intentions, etc. that are normative within that form of life and consistent with its highwater marks as found in its myths and ideology. For in a real sense, the ideological umbrella that hovers over a given form of life helps to shape and keep in perspective just what are the legitimate hopes, possibilities, dispositions and intentions.

If our procedure is correct, and we think that it is, then language which remains a human activity gets placed in a form of life—the living, operative or normative way of seeing, judging and assessing. Here, the form of life becomes something like the overriding non-linguistic grammar (logical geography that maps our way) with the final unwritten rules for deciding all disputes.

THE OVERCOME

Stated in another way, and again to remind us of the need to install key concepts in the language that we adopted without installing into it any redemptive concepts peculiar to us, language is used within the bounds of the form of life that governs the speaker. And his language, its concepts, intentions and overall consciousness of the world and life are there grounded.

This way of seeing is in ways a revision of the existentialists' point of view, in which individuals with all their activities are grounded in the context of their culture, language, custom, beliefs, hopes, system of judgment, ideologies and ways of caring and intending the world at all levels of consciousness. All these, are of course, dimensions of culture and jointly present in the form of life and the concepts of the language. Hopes, fears, beliefs and so on are all learned when one learns the concepts of a language.

And if only in this sense, the need for installing the Overcome concepts becomes important. For the nurturing that has to do with the passing on of a culture must take into account the powerful role played by learned or acquired concepts in the on-going life process of forming, framing and governing individual and corporate lives.

Our present leaning is to believe that the environment shapes and forms people. That is true to a point. We have said as much in our varied remarks about culture and form of life. But, and this is key, I am further suggesting that the concepts, in our language, play a major role in fashioning lives. As a matter of fact, I wish to further suggest that only through the mastery of the concepts in a language of a given culture, can one be effectively framed. And here, once more, is the real fear.

Blacks have indeed mastered the "I can't do this" conception as they have mastered the concept of "future Overcoming" and "future vindication." This feeds them. It is all in the concepts of their language; in the songs they sing in churches, in the sermons they hear from pulpits, and in the stories they tell which are devoid of the success/Overcome notion. And so, we become not only what we eat, but what we think and say and sing.

It should be obvious from the scheme of the argument that language is in a real sense a part of the form of life (culture). Because it is part of the form, it will be always key, and holding the final key in the liberating effort. We shall never truly be able to understand a culture without understanding the language and vice versa. And herein lies our justification for introducing linguistic analysis as basic and important in the black liberation enterprise.

In the language can be found all the concerns of the form of life; all its perplexities and woes, methods, theories about life and nature, are all there in the language. Consequently, it follows that simple forms of life have simple languages, and complex forms of life, like our own, have correlated complex languages.

The multiplicity of aspects evident in a complex form of life, like our own, requires equally multitudinous and complex concepts to express it. And because all these key elements are there, in the making of a people, attempts must be made to install whatever is needed redemptively in terms of concepts.

For as in primitive societies where views are held that would totally baffle us, but which remain conceptually right for them, so we must understand that it is the concepts about this or that way of dealing and living that frees or entraps. A good example is that which reminds us that in primitive societies certain people are witches, and magic rites and rituals are used to protect people from diseases, mental and other, and from their enemies. Rain is caused, not by meteorological conditions, but by magic rite, ghosts and gods. The people's lives are in turn constantly described and interpreted by these beliefs which are encapsulated in the concepts of the language and supported by the practices of their lives.

Western man may be inclined to think that this kind of thinking is illogical. But, this is because we have not yet grasped the force of the impact of our new way of looking at how language is integrated into the form of life. How language functions to inform, form and govern the lives of people.

If this is true of "savages," that they have a language, with a logic that explains the why of all that happens to them, then, why would it be strange for us to remind people that the same is true for all people. The concepts, the myths, the value system, everything that is important is there, resident in the language.

And, in most cases, the conceptual entrapment must

be worked on first.

Have you ever noticed how all colonials, through their missionaries, first teach their language and through the teaching of the language transmit, quietly, their form of life (the most effective way of imposing a culture); that is, a way of looking and intending, valuing and doing in the world is by transmitting the language?

Blacks would better look at this issue in the liberative effort. For as Evans-Pritchard indicates, even the magical approach of the savages is as much logical (though non-scientific) as anything else known to man. This is the case because both approaches issue from and are functions of culture. To quote:

> The fact that we attribute rain to meteorological cause alone while savages believe that gods or ghosts or magic can influence rainfall is no evidence that our brains function differently from their brains. It does not show that we 'think more logically' than savages, at least not if this expression suggests some kind of hereditary psychic superiority. It is no sign of superior intelligence on my part that I attribute rain to physical causes. I did not come to this conclusion by myself by observation and inference and have, in fact, little knowledge of the meteorological processes that lead to rain. I merely accept what everybody else in my society accepts, namely that rain is due to natural causes. This particular idea formed part of my culture long before I was born into it and little more was required of me than sufficient linguistic ability to learn it. Likewise, a savage who believes that under certain natural and ritual conditions the rainfall can be influenced by use of appropriate magic in not on account of this belief to be considered of inferior intelligence. He did not build up this belief from his observation and inferences, but adopted them in the same way as he adopted the rest of his cultural heritage, namely, by being born into it. He and I are both thinking in patterns of thought provided for us by the societies in which we live.[2]

A BLACK PASSOVER

We must note that the point being forcefully made from the above quotation is that the form of life followed in a culture, complete with its language, concepts and permissible grammar (logic) defines and limits the human's world of reality, his thoughts, his language and his cultic behaviors.

We make the mistake of believing that it is reality that gives language its meaning and point. But, Winch suggests that "reality is not what gives language sense. What is real and what is unreal and the concept of agreement with reality themselves belong to language."[3]

This is true because significant concepts in any language can only be grasped through the careful examination of the uses of those concepts within a language and a way of life.

Normally, attempts to develop concepts of reality not connected with the given and current uses in an operative language can be near impossible. For, even within primitive societies where magic is built into the form of life and the language, a coherent system of belief, with logical criteria for judgment on their authenticity forms part of the system.

There the word "magic," which would no doubt be slighted in another culture, is so commonplace that it can stand as does the word "church" in say the American culture and language. It can even prove embarrassing, like PTL, once in a while. But it goes on, as a significant part of the culture. A language in its defense can quickly be developed and accepted. And such "church" is to be found in highly developed America. Consequently, if one wishes to understand the language of magic, one must first become acculturated to the mood and waves of the culture in which magic is the norm. Apart from this, neither their way of life nor their language could be grasped.

The description of the American Indian's form of life, his ways of viewing the world, has many features common to the above description of the savages' way of life. Indians, within their form of life, classify trees as good or bad, depending on whether they are useful for firewood or other immediate human needs. Trees that cannot be useful are simply bad trees. Because of this way of seeing, a noble tree that stands gracefully in the forest (seen as beautiful to the classic tree lover) is simply bad, useless and cumbersome.

Their form of life permits no aesthetic value for trees. Another person, from another form of life, on hearing an Indian classify a beautiful oak tree as bad, could hardly understand what is meant. He may go looking for scars and other types of imperfections, but finding none, he would remain perplexed until he examines the Indian's form of life and language within which such usage is grounded.

In the same way, the Hindu starves, but reverently fattens his cow. In his language the cow is holy and set apart. This is also shown from his form of life, he starves and protects the cow. Another person can eat beef with relish and his language can say: "Beef is the best of meats." The Hindu cannot say and mean that in the same way because his form of life precludes him from using words within such form.

Black thinking, language and form of life is stuck somewhere here. The language of failure; the language of the future making things right; the language of blaming others for their plight and placing everything in environment circumstances, has a working logic that is firmly installed and that functions as the interpretive grammar of black life, hopes and behaviors.

The argument in this section would lead the reader to believe that the language and culture truly have the black man trapped and that his liberation thinkers, themselves trapped in the language and culture cannot, apart from stepping out for a while (like Moses in Midian), learn the new language that must be taught to the entrapped people.

Apart from this, the language with its "under concepts" and the form of life, existing in its "under" (oppressed mood) will remain self-perpetuating. They feed and support each other, offering the grammar and the evidence. And there is a logic to the pathology of black life, in much the same way as there is a logic to the savages' "magic," the Hindu's "holy cow" and the PTL's church.

Again we return to the one conclusion all our arguments continually force upon us, the need to install in the language of blacks the required "over" concepts and the appropriate confirming cultic ritual and story through which the concepts are to be developed and transmitted.

A BLACK PASSOVER

Apart from this, the prognosis is one that sees blacks forever speaking the same language, devoid of concepts of success and mastery, eternally hopeful, but somehow trapped in the logic and grammar of a language and life that they continue to say that they hate.

And herein lies the other problem that black leaders often allude to: the self-hate and self-destruct tendencies in black communities. Sad as it is to admit, it is the prevalent language, grammar and form of life which function in whirlwind fashion, that so successfully traps and holds the black man in a conceptual frame of mind from which he wishes so much to escape, but cannot.

Should I be right in my analysis, and I think that I am, then the way out of this conceptual entrapment for blacks is via the development or appropriation of the kinds of life-saving, life-changing concepts that can Overcome the prevailing negative ones; and these must be dramatically installed in the language, cult and form of life. Everyone must know of it. It must be accepted as a given from above, or it must be shown to have been always there, but it has gone unnoticed in recent times because of the overwhelming and taxing nature of the experience of the last 400 years.

Should we be able to install into the consciousness of all blacks, the concept that they have already "Overcome;" that is, had their Passover; should they learn to sing the Overcome hymn and see that what they had hoped for has already been "done" for them, then blacks need only to be challenged to become what we already are. And the many who are ready will surprise us all.

Like with any other redemptive movement, conceptual freedom and clarity must come first, setting as it were the parameters for the behaviors that result from the mastery of redemptive concepts.

One would have noticed that the concept of "form of life" does for the individual exactly what the concept of grammar does for language—it provides a consistent working relationship, a harmony if you will, between the world as it is intended by the people and the language used to express it. And if blacks are fed by concepts that tell them they are not ready, able, and willing; that they have none of the required competencies or propensities; if their guidance systems, their language and its concepts confirm pathology, how shall they ever emerge from it without the development of the antidote? The antidote, contrary to what black liberation thinkers have been emphasizing, is not more money, acceptance by whites, or the absence of racism, etc. Rather, it is the introduction of the concept of "the Overcome" as a done deal.

Now we must make another linguistic move and show the why of this extended argument. The notion "form of life" as used by us is not however exactly like grammar in its functioning. Grammar handles the concepts as they are taken up by the language and hence can have something of a disinterested character about it.

Grammar can permit people to talk in an "about mood" on an intellectually objective plane. Grammar can permit one to tell lies, in other words. "Form of life," while it remains essentially like grammar, strikes us as being more consistent with ways of speaking in an "of mood" that is existentially involved and tied in with levels of consciousness, intending and caring in the world.

Language, seen as part of the form of life, is more consistent with our understanding of it in the "of mood." We may appear somewhat paradoxical on this point, claiming on the one hand that form of life and language are almost identical, each reflecting the other, and on the other hand, that there are two fundamental types of language, one in the "of mood" and the other in the "about mood."

At the same time, we are suggesting that the language in the "of mood" is more closely related to the concept "form of life." The paradox, however, is more apparent than real. It was necessary to make the distinction to aid clarity. But, there is a sense in which apparently disinterested talk in an "about mood" can be viewed as being of the nature of talk in the "of mood." For whenever the descriptions and presuppositions in the "about mood" truly reflect the form of life of those involved, the paradox is resolved.

We do believe, however, that some talk, especially lifesaving redemptive talk, must always be placed in the "of mood" where it can reflect the form of life and level of consciousness, more so than in the "about mood" in which it often becomes non-consequential intellectual and disinterested linguistic games. Liberation talk, geared as it must be to the framing and forming of liberated human lives must therefore fit within the framework of talk in the "of mood." For it is only there that it can make the desired difference of framing lives.

We hardly wish to suggest that all talk in the "about mood" is intellectualistic, pedantic and non-consequential. Such can be used to get things straight, to stabilize ideologies, dogmas, theories and positions; it can also analyze them in an unprejudiced manner. However, it must be maintained that certain disciplines, liberation theology among them, are of the type that must be placed within a form of life where they can be dealt with in an "of" rather than an "about" mood.

This is the case because such remain disciplines that have as their agenda the framing, fashioning and governing of human lives.

We are suggesting that some disciplines, as aids to life, must form and direct lives, and we intend to demonstrate further that the efficacious language of the black liberation thinkers must be in the "of mood," if it is to make the desired difference of reflecting, shaping and governing the level of consciousness (way of looking caringly at our world), while it points to the way of intensifying or improving the existent form of life. There are yet many areas of life for which only a language in the "of mood" can be truly effective.

To conclude our reflections on the notion "form of life," especially as we remember that our intention is to develop the liberated, Overcoming form of life, we are reminded that the form, non-linguistic and functioning like grammar (as in speaking grammatically) is always there and mirrored in the language, even though it is often not spoken. It often includes aspects of the subjects' intentions, purposes, aims, limitations and capabilities, together with his way of looking at and intending his world.

The form of life (a negative one for blacks, according to their own descriptions) must be examined, for it is required as the necessary frame for what is said. For a man could claim with the greatest eloquence and techniques of persuasion that he "has Overcome today," but his words will remain out of place and as on the lips of the wrong speaker to his listeners, if his character, propensities, intentions and form of life do not bear out what is proclaimed.

In such a case, his words are out of place, being incorrectly placed on the wrong lips, the lips of one whose dispositional stance and behaviors nullify silently—in a non-linguistic form, all the beautiful words spoken about "Overcome/Passover." A man's activities show him to the world for what he is with greater ease and with a greater degree of accuracy than many fine words.

No wonder that the common cliches people use remain so practically forceful: "Don't tell me that you love me, show me;" "Actions speak louder than words;" "Example is better than precept." All these common proverbial sayings, which encapsulate the message and critique of the populace on the tendency to separate language from life—refusing to recognize the imperative and indicative aspects of some of the concepts in our language—can form the *modus operandi* of academicians and others who aspire to follow their ways.

The common people know that form of life is shown to others and seen easily by them and is that which offers interpretive form for the words. And this explains why whites continue to describe us collectively in negative ways. They are doing nothing more or less than what we do to ourselves. For if the subject of "the Overcome" is important, why can't the life show it?

My remarks here are not intended to discredit linguistic telling forth of the truth. That is in and of itself an important language game to be perfected and requiring real competencies. But, I do wish to indicate that the life lived, and the activities initiated, are often more instructive than the mass of words. In other words, one's life, work and activities must, as it were, bear out one's talk. And this is absolutely required in the liberation exercise, where talk without some form of living accompaniment often turns out to be mere babble.

For how liberation concepts are understood are hardly a case of words alone, since there are several language games that can only be tested and authenticated as meaningful and significant through a certain congruity between the words and what they are intended to express and the user's total life including moods, likes, abilities, leanings, tastes, dispositions, propensities, judgments and behaviors.

It should be obvious that the concept, form of life, carries with it aspects of the conventional. Hanna Pitkin's description of the term is colorful and effective. For, "Human life as we live and observe it is not just a random, continuous flow, but displays recurrent patterns, regularities, characteristic ways of doing and being, of feeling and acting, of speaking and interacting."[4]

Human life tends to form patterns which are more or less consistently trustworthy. They are like the givens or conventions of a culture. If the culture is what we like, what we wish to sustain, then the task is one of nurturing and acquainting people with, or the initiating of persons into the existing, "good" form of life.

If, however, as in the case of blacks the culture is suspect and lacking in key areas, like being devoid of success concepts, then, something more radical must be done. We develop and install the concepts and in turn teach them (with their factual, indicative, imperative and conditional nuances) to the members of the culture. We believe that liberation's chief business is one of getting people conceptually ready for thinking, hoping, and succeeding within a liberated form of life.

This is done by offering people access to the concepts that encapsulate the concerns of the form of life, access to the institutions that support, keep alive and reinforce them. It is somewhere within this process that liberated lives are formed. And, this cannot happen apart from the mastery of the concepts of the language and culture.

In a real sense, blacks remain trapped because they have been led to the mastery of a language and culture devoid of liberation, the Overcome, and success concepts.

If we are correct in believing that the concepts of a language and culture house and hold for the participants in that culture all their concerns, hopes and limitations (and we think we are right), then one should not be surprised at the trapped situation in which blacks find themselves. None of the desired liberation can even begin to happen apart from a mastery of the family of concepts, (complete with their moral imperatives) related to liberation. For it is in and through the mastery of the concepts of a culture that one Overcomes.

Chapter Nine Notes

[1] Paul L. Holmer, "About Understanding," Unpublished paper, p. 11.

[2] E. Evans-Pritchard. "Levy-Bruhl's Theory of Primitive Mentality" in Bulletin of the Faculty of Arts. University of Egypt, 1934. Cited in Peter Winch *Ethics in Action*, London: Routledge and Kegan Paul, 1972, pp. 9-10.

[3] Peter Winch, *Ethics in Action*, p. 12.

[4] Hanna Pitkin, *Wittgenstein and Justice*, Berkeley: University of California Press. 1972, p. 132.

Chapter Ten

Some Concluding Remarks

The strategic intent of this book has been, I hope, accomplished. The arguments have been varied, but all led to the conclusion that blacks must at some point claim their victories, institute them, and tell about them in story and rite...saying and doing. The story must account for all aspects of black being. It must treat slavery. But, it cannot see slavery and its resultant dehumanization as in anyway that which most formed the character of the people.

To date, in many silent ways, this is actually what is being presented.

The black story (blackstory, the history that goes with The Overcome) must begin in lofty myths about greater beginnings that gave birth to modern culture and civilization. This can be done with great ease because it also happens to be true and can be documented. Even the Ten Commandments can be shown to have originated in Africa. Moses was an African. Geometry, philosophy and even Christian philosophical theology began there with Augustine of Hippo.

Then the story of our decline must be told. It includes the horrors of dislocation; the middle passage; the dehumanization of slavery; the many struggles and revolts and attempts to escape; the Underground Railroad; abolition without support systems et al.

The story must continue with the horrors and victories; with the heroes and heroines—Dred Scott to Marcus Garvey and Malcolm X who played their various parts in the struggle. It must recount what happened when Rosa Parks, Martin Luther King, Jr., Paul Robeson, W.E.B. DuBois, and A. Philip Randolph decided to take a different stand and make some changes. The struggle, the little and big victories, must be recounted.

The story of Dr. King is to be given special significance because he was sacrificed for us. Many others died for us, including Malcolm X. But, only Dr. King was elevated. He completed the cycle. He is already the one. And, his family cannot be among those who do the interpretation of the exaltation. Their efforts through the Martin Luther King Center for Non-Violent Change are already working to break up the family as mother fights son for power. That cannot be our game. No further division, but a coming together through a common interpretation of a story that completes a major stage of struggling from "under status" to "over status" and clears the way for us, as a people, to continue the story, as an "overcoming people," the people of the "Overcome."

The Overcome must then be made to function in black life much as the Passover is made to function in Jewish life. Just as the Jews are the "Passover people," so blacks will become the "Overcome people, or the people of the Overcome." Teachings will go along with this process. Such teachings will offer a new character-resident description of blacks as people who will overcome all perplexities placed in their way because it is their new nature to do just that.

The teachings will show that blacks have overcome all perplexities placed on them. Dislocation from their homeland; negative descriptions of their color and their character; the stealing of their land, language and culture; their designation as three-fifths man; their placement in ghettos; and much, much, more. They have overcome all these and the curse of the extended experience has now been turned into a blessing. It was all these rough experiences that forged the new persona and character of the black man. He is now an overcomer, after all these years of being forced to survive against all odds. He is now like Spike Lee who dares to call his flourishing production company, "Forty Acres and a Mule."

Through this he ridicules those who refused to honor even this meager promise to get the freed blacks started.

A BLACK PASSOVER

Against the odds; without the promised forty acres and a mule, this man of the Overcome beats the oppressor at his own game. He and many others continue to find the way. And therein they demonstrate their new character...as overcomers.

The Overcome will therefore represent the event through which we are "transformed" from under to over, after reviewing all the past "inputs," from lofty beginnings, through slavery and the Civil Rights Era to the new era when we are commanded to build our own life-saving and supporting institutions.

Most of the overcoming work must be done in the next stages as we develop plans for action and strategies that would guarantee the appropriate "outcomes" that can jibe with the new status, the Overcome status.

Finally, just as Jews and Christians reinforce yearly (Jews) and weekly and even daily for some Christians their "Overcome/Passover" happening, something like a Passover rite or a Christian Mass, must be developed. Through this the significance of the Overcome will be told and developed over centuries to come. The Overcome rite could be done over a week, the week prior to April 4, each year, with different parts of the story being told to the children each night, over dinner. Then, a shortened version of the rite must be developed for use during other "rites of passage" services. These rites and the stories to go along with them are currently being developed and will be available in the near future.

Introducing the Overcome to function much as Easter and Passover function in the life of Christians and Jews has much to offer. The true significance of the Overcome will emerge after many and varied sub-concepts that point to triumphs, victories and their attendant competencies and inspirations are developed and plugged into the "mother concept," Overcome.

To hear some blacks talk, one would conclude that more education, seen as new knowledge, is all that is needed to correct the pathology in black communities. But nothing could be further from the truth.

What is needed can best be described as a conversion or turning whereby blacks are converted away from the old ways of seeing, talking and doing and transformed. This is like a process of cultivation during which time the

THE OVERCOME

true nature and impact of a concept like the Overcome is inculcated to the point at which blacks are enabled to communicate and perform as overcomers.

The Overcome then becomes not another add-on or option. It is not something blacks ought to do, may do, will do or could do. It rather describes a new being, the Overcome being, whose re-described nature forces upon him behaviors in the Overcome mode. The doing of Overcome things will occur, in time, involuntarily as such become automatic and natural.

The black man of the Overcome remains who he is, an overcomer, even when he is asleep; even when he is down for a moment. For it is this overcoming nature that will empower him to re-establish himself.

There is massive danger resident in the introduction of the concept of the Overcome as a done deal. It is given to misunderstanding as people stop short of completing the cycle. The Overcome could be grossly misunderstood.

The introduction of the concept of the Overcome to describe the true nature and character of the new black man adds a fundamental character description to the enterprise. The heart of the black Overcome ticks here. Blacks are overcomers by description and nature. In philosophy as in math, this beginning theorem is true by definition. As a circle, a square and triangle in mathematics; and as the fundamental tenets of all religions are true by definition, so too must the beginning character description of blacks as overcomers by nature be true, first, by definition. How Pygmalion!

And just as the character of a circle, square triangle and other mathematical theorems, true at first by definition, permits myriads of calculations and the consequent building of fine structures, so too will the Overcome function in the life of blacks after the establishment of the great divide of their understanding of themselves and how they stand in the world.

The Overcome is perhaps the only concept that can effectively do what I am advocating. Many people, understanding aspects of the Overcome, wish to name it the new Renaissance. Aspects of renaissance are very present in the concept of the Overcome. But that concept cannot capture and hold all aspects of the Overcome.

Overcome, with its ability to communicate disposi-

A BLACK PASSOVER

tional understandings, while permitting us to talk about overcoming activities, is historically significant. It has an historical identification with the black struggle and is consequently most appropriate. It is also a much more powerful teaching concept.

The Overcome could also be introduced in other ways.

It could be shown that it is the historical nature of blacks to overcome whatever their oppressors place on them. Did we not overcome our separation from Africa? Did we not overcome the Middle Passage? Did we not overcome the horrors of slavery? Did we not overcome Dred Scott setbacks? Yes. We did through the blood of our foreparents. They overcame in worse times and under much worse conditions, harsher realities. Their corporate overcoming forged our new characters. We are now, whether we accept it willingly or not, the people of the Overcome.

The procedure for the future will go something like this. Whenever the concentrated pressures of racism, black on black hate and crime; poverty or whatever is negative comes upon us whether as society or as individuals, the blacks of the Overcome will remind themselves: Our foreparents forged for us the character of overcomers. Pressures will come...pressure as on coal. Pressure on coal makes dust or forges diamonds. Diamonds or dust? We will be the diamonds. We will overcome whatever is placed in our way because it is our nature to do this; and we owe it to our forebears.

Appendix A

King: Making His Myth
The Baltimore Times
Volume 2, No. 3, January, 1988

As we celebrate the birthday of Martin Luther King, Jr., the first authentic black martyr—with a national holiday during the month of January—it is fitting that we should assess the development of the interpretive story—the myth and its meaning.

All peoples need their significant historical and mythological heroes. Often, the historic and mythical aspects are neatly combined for effect. Blacks in America may need to start developing the larger than life interpretive, easy- to-tell and remember, significant stories about their historic hero and martyr, Dr. King.

To date, there is no such story that could go with MLK's national holiday. There are themes such as that "about making the dream a reality." Other themes will emerge. We believe that much as dear and larger than life stories were developed about the father of America, General George Washington, the one who never told a lie. Remember that "cherry tree"? Then, so too, our storytellers must get to the work of lifting Martin Luther King to the level of George Washington, the other American who has a national holiday named in his honor.

The real significance of MLK's elevation to a place equal to George Washington has not yet been explored or expressed. It appears to us as though the larger American society, through the celebration of Martin Luther King's birthday, is declaring that it has done all it could in the symbolic area. And it has. All black Americans have symbolic parity with white Americans. Black America must now do much of the rest of the work itself. It must take the ball and run for the touchdown.

We hope that the redemptive significance of MLK's life, death, and message will emerge as blacks recognize that through Dr. King's elevation, on the national level, to parity with "father" George Washington, intentionally or unintentionally, equity (symbolic) has been established as the national policy. Equality is "installed" on the national level. Things can never be the same again! Equality needs only to be made real. Only the concerted efforts of blacks can make this real. Only blacks can do this. And they shall. Thanks Martin. Happy Birthday.

A BLACK PASSOVER

Appendix B

Towards A Victory Song
The Baltimore Times
Volume 2, No. 2, December, 1987

Jesse Jackson is currently leading the pack of Democrats running for the presidency. He continues to have the widest name recognition. He is a gifted candidate, certainly he is the most articulate and hell-bent on demonstrating that a black man could mount a credible race for the presidency, and with the intention of winning and doing a good job. He wants to become president of all the people.

Whether Jesse wins or not, a valuable lesson is being taught. The black man's place in this country need not be on the street corners or the penitentiary. For without a law degree or high-powered profession (just a Reverend), Jesse is showing the way. If he can, so can you.

Whites need not fear Jesse or other black politicians. They know and note (one pointed this out to me the other day) that blacks in power lean over backwards to show they are not racists. As a matter of fact, blacks are the only true Americans at heart. Others are Polish, Jewish, or Italians first.

A look at any government agency headed by blacks—city, state or federal—will demonstrate that without fail the black "chief" will place mostly whites. This is one reason for large companies hiring blacks as personnel directors. This for them has proven the surest way of keeping the masses of blacks in their place.

But as we move into a future in which blacks identify and celebrate their Overcoming/Passover through Dr. Martin Luther King, Jr., the vindicated and elevated one, this will change.

Think just how strange and odd it will be for Jesse Jackson to win the presidency and on Inauguration Day strike up the band to lead us in song: "We Shall Overcome Someday!"

What shall be made to count as criteria for overcoming? When and through what is the strife over and the battle done? Would Jesse, as president, do it? Would Mr. Adams, the multi-millionaire, do it? Can the black owners of Beatrice Foods signal it? Could our corporate support of Harbor Bank, giving it our first $100,000 in savings, covered by the U.S. government, same as every other bank, do it?

It would appear to us that prior to winning the election, black Americans had better learn the Overcome victory song. For something, some victory, some elevation must sooner or later be used as the black Waterloo, the black Fourth of July, establishing for all times the before and after interpretive handle for dealing with black failures and successes. This is indeed necessary if black successes are not forever to be seen as peculiarities, but as essentially indicative of our true nature.

Jesse might just win. He is the brightest of the lot. But when he wins, our song must be the victory song, "We Have Overcome Today."

And if he loses, the song does not change. Kennedy, Hart and Biden, each in his own time did lose, but the general description of their people as "over" has not changed.

Another simply steps in to continue the series.

A BLACK PASSOVER

Appendix C

Happy Passover, Easter, Overcome
The Baltimore Times,
Volume 2, No. 6, April, 1988

A blessed Easter, Overcome, Passover, Spring to all our readers. This year, for some perhaps cosmic reasons, Spring, Passover and Easter arrived at the same time to celebrate the rebirth of nature after the Winter hiatus. Time for Jews to celebrate and recall the Passover (bridge) from bondage to freedom and time for Christians to celebrate and recall that even though Jesus was killed on Good Friday, He has somehow through the power of God, overcome negativity and death, and the festive songs of triumph, victory and exulting, must begin at sunrise on Easter Day.

Have blacks noticed how nature (through Spring); Jews (through Passover); Christians (through Easter) celebrate and gain strength to go on rejuvenating, exulting while at the same time managing pain, failure, war, perplexity and pathology—all conditions of humans that are transfield and transcultural, in essence touching all human souls? We hope so. For this year, for some strange cosmic reasons, Good Friday, Passover, Easter and the assassination of Martin Luther King, Jr. follow each other, day after day in perfect sequence. We do not know when this will ever happen again. But twenty years after the death of MLK, and three years after his vindication and elevation, (like resurrection) history chooses to line up Good Friday, Passover, Easter and MLK's death day (April 4).

Also, a local priest has declared black Overcome Day that will function as the black Overcoming/Passover, through the life, ministry, death and consequent elevation of Martin Luther King, Jr.

Cosmic forces are today lending Father Peter Bramble, rector of St. Katherine's Episcopal Church in Baltimore, a hand as he continues to preach the black Overcome/Passover through MLK.

The priest who recalls that at every Mass he says, "Christ our passover is sacrificed for us, therefore let us keep the feast" (1 Cor. 5:7–8), is certain that God wants blacks to establish the interpretive page break, the

THE OVERCOME

before/after of being under/over and celebrate what has been already done. The victory has been installed in the American body of informative conventions. Absolute equality, through Martin Luther King, Jr., who holds a status equal to George Washington, the father of the nation, is cause for exulting and the emergence of triumphalism in the culture.

At this beginning stage, Father Bramble urges all blacks to do a simple Overcome rite individually, in family, at church, in sorority or on street corners by simply singing these words: "We Have Overcome, We Have Overcome, We Have Overcome Today. O Deep In Our Hearts, We Do Proclaim, We Have Overcome Today."

Each year, as the early morning ritual to go along with other prayers and thanksgivings on the death date of MLK, do the same...and so experience some of what keeps the Easter festival triumphant and the Jews' Passover meaningful and alive.

Father Bramble just might be correct. The cosmic bringing together of Spring, Good Friday, Passover, Easter and black Overcome Day (April 4) days stacked in perfect sequence has now authenticated the prophetic call of one in our midst. The instituting of the rite and festival is all that is now left. Happy Passover, Easter and Overcome to Baltimore and America!

A BLACK PASSOVER

Appendix D

MLK's Life: A Bridge
The Baltimore Times, January 16, 1989

The common man is heeding the call for the black Overcome. He is understanding the strategic necessity. But the black leadership is opting to keep him from waking up to the reality of the "now" and "not-yet" aspects of any liberative process. In a time when so much is made of the "not yet" or futuristic aspects of liberation—pie in the sky when you die—equal emphasis must be placed on the already accomplished. For both of these aspects of the total process must be made to stand in creative tension.

So many black leaders and preachers continue to talk and preach as though there have been no major victories; nothing to celebrate along the way. And that is a lie. The kind of lie that breeds apathy. Don't they understand that if prolonged struggle brings no victories, the fighters tire and die in time. Must the current black leadership die before a corporate victory, a genesis victory in which they all had a hand and played a major part, can be declared?

The Black Overcome, through the death and elevation of Dr. King, is. It need not be declared again. But it must be installed in the consciousness of blacks all over the world. And not as a statement of completion or consummation, but as inauguration. This must be done in the recognition of the fact that the very black leaders who are aging now and resisting the introduction of the Black Overcome as our corporate beginning victory story are the ones with the most to lose. For they are in fact telling their children that their marching, going to jail and protesting was in vain.

But their action which culminated in the death and elevation of Martin Luther King brought us thus far, over the bridge! Those who resist making Dr. King's life, death, and elevation function in our lives like the Fourth of July or Easter are saying that he accomplished little. And that is a dysfunctional lie. He at least elevated the black man to the same level as George Washington, the father of the nation.

I say that he did much by dying. The Congressional Black Caucus did much when it elevated Dr. King thereby forcing the nation to vindicate his cause and ours. Those who walked with him helped to create this Overcome event. And we must name it as such and lock it in history with redemptive meaning. That is good news for a people told often by their preachers that they are losers. A people made to celebrate Jubilee with sad songs!

People fight and die to protect what they have, even concepts, rites and myths. But if black leaders continue to preach that all successes are in the future, with no corporate victory that can take us over, they are in fact feeding apathy. What's the use!

And so, once more as we celebrate the birth, life, ministry, death, elevation and vindication of The King we recognize our conceptual overcoming in the first instance, and we resolve to spend the rest of our lives effectuating what already is. We believe that in Dr. King our overcoming is fulfilled though yet to be consummated. Isn't that good news? He did not just give us a dream. He gave us his blood. He gave us his life to serve as the bridge, the overcoming bridge. He is the Black Overcome. Let us name it. Let us celebrate it. Let us live to make it real so that his dying will not be in vain. Thanks Martin. Happy Birthday.

A BLACK PASSOVER

Appendix E

What's in a Name?
The Baltimore Times, January 16, 1989

Since 1963, the black peoples of America have had a crisis in identity. They seem not to know the name by which they will be called.

They have been called colored, Negro, minority, black, Afro and American. In recent weeks, Jesse Jackson, a leader in his own right, asked this nameless people to choose yet another name. The new name: African-American. (But this is not even new. Remember the AME Church!)

What are others to think of a people with no name; a people whose very name is in process? A people who have changed names six to seven times in fewer than 50 years have a real problem. It is simple: no name, no character. Naming locks in character. Naming, usually done during the participation in and celebration of the first rite of passage, is usually the first "done deal" along life's way.

Are black leaders and change agents against the installation of any done deals? Are such leaders really unaware of the fact that the fighting of the same battle over and over again without ever declaring victory and naming and dating the victorious battle is self-defeating? Are they aware that such is the source of the apathy that shows itself in anger against our leading organizations and our leaders? And will it be that even the naming of this people "shall happen someday"? Will there ever be any done deals in the thinking of black people?

Blacks would better win the naming battle at some time. If black and proud, so be it. If colored or Negro, Afro or African, please settle on the name so that we can at least know whose mighty deeds are to be recorded and whose history we are participating in making.

The current black naming problem remains conceptual at the core. The inability to name and accept the name is one more sign that the people are not together in any sense, for if there is not even unity in the naming, how can there be any unity in the story, the strategy and the Vision Glorious?

THE OVERCOME

Appendix F

Naming Ourselves
The Baltimore Times
August 3, 1989

The black leadership is making its most terrible mistake yet. Since Jesse Jackson called that ill-advised African-American get-together, a gathering that did nothing but rehash old agendas, blacks have been calling themselves African-Americans.

Changing a name once or twice for meaning is OK. Changing your name seven times in less than 20 years points to a conceptual problem. A name still locks in history, experiences and character.

Blacks have been called or have called themselves so many names over the last 20 years that few know what is truly permissible. They have been Negro (MLK's word) colored, Afro, black and now African. Those who argue for the new designation base their arguments on solid ground. Land of origin is important. But, no victories have been won by African-Americans. The victories were won as blacks. The current move is nothing short of one that would effectively abandon the successes as they seek to run away from the psychological problems they really do have with being called black.

The trick and secret of overcoming reside in the acts through which an under group takes exactly that which is used to "down" them and elevates and exalts the same. In short, lift it up in the face of those who use it to down us.

When in the 1960's Negroes, who were publicly ashamed to be called blacks, turned the conceptual tables on the oppressors and virtually laughed at them by responding, "Say it loud, I'm black and I'm proud," the first major victory was won by blacks.

The oppressor did not know how to get around that one. For Christians, the reminder comes in contemplating that Jesus was "downed" with the cross. The initial response was "Let's go fishing." Then, some smart aleck introduced the concept of overcoming death through the cross—"In the cross of Christ I glory." The downer was made into an upper, and the victory was won. Two thousand years later, Jesus still saves, as the black preacher proudly proclaims.

The trick is to turn the symbol of embarrassment into the symbol of victory. Until that is truly done, there is no victory. The blacks of the 1960's succeeded in doing this. Those of the 1980's continue to dismantle victories and institutions handed down as each new generation tries to rediscover the wheel, starting from scratch as they rename themselves.

Pity us if we do not claim and install our victories. Pity us if we rename ourselves in every generation. Pity us if no corporate story is ever developed around a victorious name.

I happen to believe that since our victories were won through the name black, we should never change.

I will always be proudly, competently, beautifully and ably black and African.

I will never devalue blackness to emphasize African or vice versa. We are both/and much, much more.

Blacks, whatever you do, remember that whites remain white and German or Italian.

My prayer is that we will grow up conceptually and accept all that we are...especially that which we will take to the grave with us.

Be black and proud. Be African and proud. Get a touch of the white man's both/and philosophy.

THE OVERCOME

Appendix G
The Overcome by R. B. Jones
The Baltimore Times,
July 3, 1989

Prophetic visions are like flashes of lightning across a darkened sky. These are natural events that illuminate the path of human development just when the darkness seems to dominate. Father Peter Bramble, pastor of St. Katherine's Episcopal Church in Baltimore, has had a prophetic vision about the condition of black people in the United States.

He is one of a long line of prophets who have meditated on the dilemma and proposed bold and sometimes frightening solutions. In 1831, Prophet Nat Turner received revelations from God that slavery's immense evils could only be ended through a massive blood sacrifice. Turner led the largest slave revolt in U.S. history. Though his rebellion did not end slavery, it left his confession which was an indictment of slavery and a warning that chilled the blood of the slaveholders. In the midst of slavery, Turner asserted that God spoke to a slave.

Bishop Henry McNeal Turner of the African Methodist Episcopal Church boldly declared that God is black at the turn of the century when black people were suffering the blows of segregation, lynching and the loss of the vote. Bishop Turner said that every group of people sees God in their own image, and it is only proper that black people see God in their own image.

In the midst of despair and oppression, Bishop Turner told black people to look at themselves and see God.

Father Bramble is an heir to Turner's legacy of prophetic vision. He has boldly declared that black people have already overcome and no longer need to sing, "We Shall Overcome Someday."

Using the sacrificial life, death and consequent elevation of Dr. Martin Luther King, Jr. as the symbol, sign and marker, Father Bramble shows that black people in America have triumphed without realizing their victory. The realization, according to Bramble, will come when the victory is named and placed, and when a ritualistic day that recalls the significance of the victory is institutional-

A BLACK PASSOVER

ized in the black community. The Overcome will banish the victim imagery from being the primary life-forming imagery in the minds of blacks because it will illustrate in a forceful way a corporate triumph over oppression and defeat.

The symbol, Martin Luther King, Jr., was a man who rose to world-wide prominence as the embodiment of the struggle of black people in this country. He too was a man with a prophetic vision that many people in the society opposed bitterly. Yet, with an unrelenting faith in the inevitability of his vision, Dr. King saw the "Promised Land." An assassin's bullet killed the man, but not the prophetic vision. The assassin's bullet actually ushered in the Black Overcome, according to Bramble.

Dr. King's birthday became a national holiday, an honor unsurpassed in this nation. This came to pass through the efforts of the black community (through men like Parren J. Mitchell, a member of Father Bramble's church) against the wishes of powerful people like President Ronald Reagan and other traditional power-brokers. This act by itself symbolizes the fact that black people have already overcome. Their leaders and most of the people have not yet realized that through these happenings they have gone from being always "under," slaves/second class citizens, to "over"—empowered and exalted through the accomplishments of Dr. King. Their new status remains only to be claimed, instituted and lived out.

Father Bramble, with great insight, points out that the difference between the black and Jewish communities, which both have a history of oppression, is that Jews have corporate (shared by all, like Passover) rituals that enable them to recall and participate in their common triumph over oppression from generation to generation.

With Overcome, as described and defined by Father Bramble's prophetic work, black people will realize their triumph and its corporate value and will incorporate it into the body of life-forming and life-governing concepts. They will in time institute the needed Overcome ritual (not as prayer breakfasts) that will enable present and future generations to live victorious—Overcome—lives.

In the midst of pathology, Father Bramble proclaims the Black Overcome. Paradox and challenge.